Contents

About this guide

Designing for Accessibility is part of a new generation of design guides jointly published by CAE and RIBA Enterprises. The series articulates our joint commitment to environments designed to include the requirements of all users. Design guidance in the series is based on relevant legislation, acknowledged good practice deriving from user experience, good design, and, where possible, empirical research. The CAE/RIBA Enterprises series will assist service providers, employers and education providers seeking to fulfil their duties under the Disability Discrimination Act 1995. It will also aid those responsible for the development of the built environment and those who use it, which can include architects, designers, facilities managers, and a range of consumers including disabled people.

Guidance contained in *Designing for Accessibility* is based primarily on the 2004 edition of the Approved Document for Part M of the Building Regulations (AD M), with additional material from British Standard BS 8300:2001 *Design of buildings and their approaches to meet the needs of disabled people – Code of practice* and from the accumulated experience of good design practice.

Designing for Accessibility is about helping to achieve good practice. Some of the recommendations contained in it are not requirements under AD M or specified in the British Standard. Architects and designers should refer directly to these documents in addition to using *Designing for Accessibility*, which provides a context within which to apply design guidance. Inclusive design is a fast-moving field, and there will be further changes in legislation, about which service providers, facilities managers, architects and designers will need to keep themselves informed.

Designing for Accessibility covers features that commonly occur in a wide range of public buildings. It does not cover: audience and spectator seating; refreshment facilities; sleeping accommodation; changing and shower facilities and bathrooms; or guidance that refers to specific building types. Where references are made to other sources of guidance, details of these can be found in Appendix one.

While *Designing for Accessibility* has no legal status, an architect's or designer's duty of care to a client will be demonstrated by following good practice guidance contained in it.

The legislative framework

Building Regulations

In England and Wales, building design and construction is governed by the Building Regulations (see p 4 for Scotland and Northern Ireland). These regulations comprise a series of requirements for specific purposes: health and safety, energy conservation, prevention of contamination of water and the welfare and convenience of persons in or about buildings.

Part M

Part M of the regulations sets minimum legal standards for access and use of buildings by all building users, including disabled people. Since a requirement for access was first introduced in 1985, there have been a number of changes to and extensions in the scope of access regulations. The most recent – and most radical – revision comes into effect on 1 May 2004. Whereas previously, Part M was concerned with 'access for disabled people', now the requirement (for non-domestic buildings) is simply that:

- **Access and use**
  'Reasonable provision shall be made for people to gain access to and use the building and its facilities'
  This does not apply to any part of a building that is used solely to enable the building or any service or fitting within the building to be inspected, repaired or maintained.

- **Access to extensions to buildings**
  'Suitable independent access shall be provided to the extension where reasonably practicable'
  This does not apply where suitable access to the extension is provided throughout the building that is extended.

- **Sanitary conveniences in extensions to buildings**
  'If sanitary conveniences are provided in any building that is to be extended, reasonable provision shall be made within the extension for sanitary conveniences'
  This does not apply where there is reasonable provision for sanitary conveniences elsewhere in the building that can be accessed by building users.

The regulation avoids specific reference to, and a definition of, disabled people. This inclusive approach means that buildings and their facilities should be accessible and usable by *all* people who use buildings – including parents with children, older people and people with disabilities.

Previously, Part M covered new buildings and extensions to existing buildings. The 2004 revision brings Part M into line with other parts of the Building Regulations by extending its scope to include alterations to existing buildings and certain changes of use.

Approved Document M

Building Regulations are supported by 'Approved Documents' which give practical guidance with respect to the regulations. While their use is not mandatory – and the requirements of regulations can be met in other ways – Approved Documents are used as a benchmark by the local authority.

The new Approved Document M (AD M), published in November 2003, offers technical guidance on providing access to and within buildings. It is informed by the relevant British Standard (BS 8300:2001 *Design of buildings and their approaches to meet the needs of*

Building Regulations

disabled people – Code of practice, see p 6), although the British Standard also contains guidance on issues that are not appropriate or realistic to control under Building Regulations approval and inspection procedures, such as interior decoration and the selection of door ironmongery. Dimensional criteria in the new AD M are largely in accordance with BS 8300. Where there are differences, these result from accumulated experience fed back to the Government during its consultation on the new AD M, and this should be followed in preference to dimensional criteria in BS 8300.

It is important that reference is made to AD M for details of the circumstances in which Part M applies and what provision is required.

Historic buildings

Since alterations to existing buildings are now covered by Part M, more historic buildings will now be affected. In recognising the need to conserve the special characteristics of historic buildings, AD M states that 'the aim should be to improve accessibility where and to the extent to which it is practically possible, always provided that the work does not prejudice the character of the historic building, or increase the risk of long-term deterioration of the building fabric or fittings'.

The role of Access Statements

Approved Document M recommends that Access Statements be provided to assist building control officers in making judgements about whether proposals make reasonable provision. Access Statements are particularly valuable where:

- the applicant chooses to meet the requirements of Part M by means other than those described in the Approved Document

- in the case of alterations to or changes of use in existing buildings, it is not practical or reasonable to achieve the level of access provision normally required

See p 5 Access Statements.

Scotland

In Scotland, access requirements are integrated into general Technical Standards. These apply to: new buildings; conversions; extensions to existing buildings (but not to the existing buildings themselves); and parts of a building that are altered or that are adversely affected by an alteration being carried out elsewhere in the building. At the time of writing, the Building Regulations system is being modernised and Technical Standards are being reviewed.
See www.scotland.gov.uk/build_regs

Northern Ireland

In Northern Ireland, Part R of the Building Regulations (NI) covers Access and Facilities for Disabled People, and is supported by Technical Booklet R:2000 (both downloadable from www2.dfpni.gov.uk).

Access Statements

An Access Statement is a description of how inclusive design principles and practice can be incorporated into a particular project or development, and subsequently maintained and managed. An Access Statement is not a static document but a living process which evolves with the scheme, from initially being fairly generic to becoming gradually more specific and detailed. Access Statements will be of benefit and relevance to the designers, contractors, planning, building control and access officers, building owners and managers and local access groups.

Access Statements have been used successfully for some time in planning applications for large, high-profile schemes. The use of Access Statements is now formally recommended in *Planning and Access for Disabled People – A Good Practice Guide* on how to ensure that the town and country planning system in England successfully and consistently delivers inclusive environments as an integral part of the development process. Published in 2003 by the Office of the Deputy Prime Minister (ODPM), the guide encourages the provision of Access Statements at the planning application stage to identify the philosophy and approach to inclusive design adopted, the key issues of the particular scheme, and the sources of advice and guidance used. An Access Statement provided for Building Regulations purposes should be seen as complementary to, and as a development of, that which is provided for planning purposes, rather than as a separate document.

An Access Statement provides an audit trail to demonstrate whether particular matters have been considered adequately and with the benefit of current and authoritative guidance. Their use can help guard against the danger of routine maintenance or minor alterations compromising access provisions that have been designed in.

Access Statements are particularly valuable where design solutions vary from those contained in AD M, but will be useful tools in all buildings. In the case of existing buildings, particularly historic buildings, such a statement will allow the designer or developer to identify the constraints posed by the existing structure and its immediate environment and to propose compensatory measures where full access proves to be impracticable or only achievable at disproportionate cost. This will also allow for justification to be provided and assessed in situations where a design solution does not meet the requirements of Part M or conform to the minimal guidance in AD M.

It will be beneficial to maintain and update Access Statements as the design progresses in order to provide the end-user of the building, who may have ongoing obligations under the DDA, with a record of the evolution of design and management decisions. Access Statements may inform future access audits, plans and strategies (see p 12). See *Planning and Access for Disabled People – A Good Practice Guide*, published by ODPM, and forthcoming guidance on Access Statements, to be published by the Disability Rights Commission, CAE and RIBA Enterprises.

British Standard BS 8300

BS 8300:2001 *Design of buildings and their approaches to meet the needs of disabled people – Code of practice* explains how the built environment can be designed to anticipate and overcome restrictions that prevent disabled people from making full use of premises and their surroundings.

Many of the design recommendations in BS 8300 are based for the first time on ergonomic research commissioned in 1997 and 2001 by the Department of the Environment, Transport and the Regions. BS 8300 includes commentary which provides a context and rationale for the design guidance. Management and maintenance issues are incorporated in recognition that these play an essential part in ensuring the accessibility of services and facilities to disabled people.

The recommendations in the standard apply to car parking provision, setting-down points and garaging, access routes to and around all buildings, and entrances to and interiors of new buildings. They inform the design guidance in the Approved Document M (AD M) of the Building Regulations. They may also be used to assess the accessibility and usability of existing buildings and, where practicable, as a basis for their improvement.

Disability Discrimination Act 1995

The Disability Discrimination Act (DDA) introduced new measures aimed at ending the discrimination which many disabled people face. In addition to granting new rights to disabled people, the Act also places duties on, among others, employers (Part 2), providers of goods, facilities and services (Part 3) and education providers (Part 4).

The main thrust of the legislation is to improve access for disabled people to employment, education and services. While the DDA does not *directly* require accessible environments to be provided for disabled people, either in their place of work or for access to goods, facilities, or services (for example in shops, restaurants or offices to which the public have access), duties under the Act include the requirement to consider barriers created by physical features of buildings and to make adjustments in certain circumstances.

The Act defines a disabled person as 'someone who has a physical or mental impairment which has a substantial and long-term adverse effect on his or her ability to carry out normal day-to-day activities'. Discrimination occurs where without justification, and for a reason which relates to the disabled person's disability, a disabled person is treated less favourably than others to whom the reason does not or would not apply.

Discrimination may also occur when there is a duty to make a reasonable adjustment and any failure to meet that duty cannot be justified.

Each Part of the DDA is supported by one or more Codes of Practice which give guidance on how to meet duties under the Act. While Codes of Practice neither impose legal obligations nor are authoritative statements of the law, they may be referred to in any legal proceedings pursued under the Act.

Building designers, while not legally required to respond to the DDA, should anticipate the requirements of the Act by presuming that employees, students and customers will fit the definition of 'disabled person' under the Act, and design buildings accordingly. Those commissioning new buildings or adaptations to existing buildings should consider the implications of the DDA in terms of their ability to employ and offer services to disabled people on an equal basis.

The DDA applies to the whole of the UK, including (with modifications) Northern Ireland.

DDA Part 2: Employment

Duties in Part 2 of the DDA covering employers were introduced in December 1996. They are amended under the Equal Treatment Directive, which implements obligations placed by the European Union on the UK in relation to disability discrimination and which comes into effect on 1 October 2004. The Directive brings into effect:

- the removal of the existing exemption for small employers (of less than 15 people)

- a significant change in the relationship between Building Regulations and Part 2 of the DDA (see below)

Also on 1 October 2004, the two existing Part 2 Codes of Practice (for employers and trade organisations) are to be replaced by two new Codes of Practice (for employment and occupation and for trade organisations and qualifying bodies).

Employers have a duty not to treat disabled people less favourably than others for a reason relating to their disability, unless this can be justified, and to make adjustments to assist disabled employees or applicants for employment. This may involve changing physical features of the premises if these put a disabled person at a substantial disadvantage in comparison with persons who are not disabled. The duty of provision of a reasonable adjustment is triggered when an individual disabled person applies for a job, is employed or it becomes apparent that an existing employee requires some form of adjustment: there is no general or anticipatory duty under Part 2 to make provision for disabled people.

There is no minimum standard of adjustment to premises required by the DDA, but the *Code of Practice for the Elimination of Discrimination in the field of Employment against Disabled Persons or Persons who have had a Disability* states that 'an employer might have to make structural or other changes such as: widening a doorway, providing a ramp or moving furniture for a wheelchair user; relocating light switches, door handles or shelves for someone who has difficulty reaching; providing appropriate contrast in décor to help the safe mobility of a visually impaired person.'

How do Building Regulations affect reasonable adjustments under Part 2?

Until 1 October 2004, an employer does not have to alter any physical characteristics of the building or extension which still complies with the Building Regulations in force at the time the building works were carried out – that is, a building or an extension to a building constructed in accordance with Part M of the Building Regulations (Part T or Technical Standards in Scotland and Part R in Northern Ireland). From 1 October 2004, this exemption is withdrawn, but an employer will still only be under an obligation to make adjustments if it is reasonable in the circumstances to do so.

DDA Part 3: Service provision

Part 3 of the DDA places duties on those providing goods, facilities or services to the public ('service providers') and those selling, letting or managing premises. The Act makes it unlawful for service providers, landlords and other persons to discriminate against disabled people in certain circumstances.

The duties on service providers are being introduced in three stages:

- since **December 1996,** it has been unlawful for service providers to treat disabled people less favourably for a reason related to their disability

- since **October 1999,** service providers have had to make 'reasonable adjustments' for disabled people, such as providing extra help or making changes to the way they provide their services, or overcoming physical barriers by providing a service by a reasonable alternative method

- from **October 2004,** service providers may have to make other 'reasonable adjustments' in relation to the physical features of their premises to overcome physical barriers to access

In considering whether or not a service provider has taken reasonable steps to comply with its duties after 1 October 2004, a court might take into account the time that the service provider has had prior to that date to make preparations.

The *Code of Practice Rights of Access: Goods, Facilities, Services and Premises,* published by the Disability Rights Commission in 2002, outlines what may be considered as reasonable for disabled people to establish rights of access to goods, facilities, services and premises. Several factors have a bearing on whether a change is a reasonable one

to make: effectiveness; practicality; cost and disruption; and financial resources. The Code of Practice gives detailed guidance on what 'reasonable adjustments' service providers are likely to have to make in three main areas of practices, policies and procedures; the provision of auxiliary aids and services; and overcoming barriers created by physical features of premises.

While the Act does not require a service provider to adopt any particular way of meeting its obligations, the Code of Practice recommends that service providers should first consider whether any physical features which create a barrier for disabled people can be removed or altered; if this is not possible, then they should consider providing a reasonable means of avoiding the physical feature; and if this is not possible either, then they should provide a reasonable alternative method of making the service available to disabled people.

How do Building Regulations affect reasonable adjustments under Part 3?
The broad principle is that if a building (or feature within a building) has been designed and constructed in such as way that it met the relevant access requirements at the time and is less than ten years old, service providers will be exempt from their requirement under the DDA to make adjustments to those physical features of their buildings covered by access regulations. The exemption relates only to the particular aspect of the physical feature in question and not to the building as a whole. The service provider may still, however, be required to provide a reasonable means of avoiding a feature or a reasonable alternative means of making services available. The exemption applies only to physical features constructed or installed in

DDA Part 3: Service provision

accordance with the 1992 or 1999 editions of Part M. Any building works undertaken before 1 October 1994 will not be protected by the exemption. At publication of the 2004 edition of AD M, the Government was still considering whether to extend the exemption to this edition.

For more detailed guidance on the inter-relationship between Building Regulations and the DDA and on the issue of leases and the DDA, see section 6 of the Part 3 Code of Practice.

How can service providers identify possible adjustments?
Service providers are more likely to be able to comply with their 'general', 'evolving' and 'anticipatory' duty to make adjustments in relation to physical features of existing buildings if they arrange for an access audit of their premises to be conducted and draw up an access plan or strategy (see p 12).

DDA Part 4: Education

When the DDA was introduced in 1995, duties on education providers in Part 4 were minimal. The Special Educational Needs and Disability Act 2001 (SENDA) amended Part 4 of the DDA and expanded the duties relating to disabled pupils and students. It also removed the exemption of publicly funded education from Part 3 of the Act (although, where a duty under Part 4 applies, Part 3 cannot apply).

Education providers are now required to make 'reasonable adjustments' for disabled students and pupils. The duties include all areas of education, schools, colleges, universities, adult education and youth services, including:

- not to treat disabled students or pupils less favourably than non-disabled students or pupils without justification

- to make reasonable adjustments to policies, practices and procedures that may discriminate against disabled students or pupils

- to provide education by a 'reasonable alternative means' where a physical feature places a disabled student/pupil at a substantial disadvantage

- a duty on local education authorities in England and Wales to plan strategically and increase the overall accessibility to school premises and the curriculum (a similar duty is placed on authorities in Scotland under the Education (Disability Strategies and Pupils' Education Records) (Scotland) Act 2002)

Additional duties placed on providers of post-16 education are as follows:

- **from September 2002:** not to discriminate against existing and prospective disabled students by treating them less favourably in the provision of student services

- **from September 2003:** to make reasonable adjustments to provide auxiliary aids

- **from September 2005:** to make adjustments to physical features. This is an anticipatory and continuing duty

Many schools or further/higher education providers are also service providers (for example, where premises are used for evening classes, exhibitions or parents' evenings) and therefore also have duties under Part 3.

Access audits, access plans and access strategies

Access audits give a 'snapshot' of an existing building at one point in time. They are a useful starting point in assessing the current state of accessibility and usability of existing buildings. Buildings which are designed or adapted with the access needs of disabled people in mind are likely to be more flexible and make it easier for employers and service providers to meet the requirements of the DDA. An access audit can form the basis of an ongoing access action plan.

CAE's film *Access Audits: a planning tool for businesses* uses a case-study approach to explain what an access audit is and how its recommendations can be used to improve a business's premises and customer service.

Access plans or **access strategies** are the best way of ensuring that the information gathered and recommendations made in the access audit are effectively used. The plan or strategy should include regular monitoring and updating of the audit, since even without major structural adaptations, buildings and the way they are used change over time. Access plans or strategies take a long-term view of improving access and identify opportunities for change (for example, at routine maintenance or when a major refit is planned), demonstrating a serious commitment to making buildings more accessible to everyone. They should include policies, procedures, practices and management; provision of equipment and auxiliary aids; and the physical environment.

The *Code of Practice Rights of Access: Goods, Facilities, Services and Premises* gives the following guidance to service providers on how they can identify possible adjustments to physical features of their buildings and reduce the likelihood of cases being brought against employers and service providers under the DDA (paragraphs 5.42 and 5.43):

'Service providers are more likely to be able to comply with their duty to make adjustments in relation to physical features if they arrange for an access audit of their premises to be conducted and draw up an access plan or strategy. Acting on the results of such an evaluation may reduce the likelihood of legal claims against the service provider.

In carrying out an audit, it is recommended that service providers seek the views of people with different disabilities, or those representing them, to assist in identifying barriers and developing effective solutions. Service providers can also draw on the extensive experience of local and national disability groups or organisations of disabled people.'

Car parking

Cars are the only practical method of transport for some disabled people, and accessible parking is therefore an important consideration. The level of provision will depend on many factors including location and use of the building. Parking bays with additional transfer space are required to allow people with reduced mobility to get into and out of their cars with the minimum of difficulty. Where on-site parking is not available, good practice would suggest maintaining a record of nearby accessible bays. In addition, an approach could be made to the local authority for the provision of on-street parking.

- Where parking is provided, at least one bay designated for disabled people should be provided as close as possible to the principal entrance of the building (see table opposite for guidance on number of bays). There are circumstances where, even when there is no standard parking provision, accessible parking may be needed.

Minimum recommended number of bays in off-street car parks
Car park used for:
Workplaces
Where the number of disabled employees is known:
One space for each known disabled employee plus one space or 2% of total capacity (whichever is greater) for visiting disabled motorists
or
Where the number of disabled employees is not known:
At least one space or 5% of the total parking capacity, whichever is the greater
Shopping, recreation and leisure facilities Minimum one space for each employee who is a disabled motorist plus 6% of the total capacity for visiting disabled motorists
Sport England recommends 8% for some sports facilities and for 50m swimming pools
Based on BS 8300

Figure 1
Designated off-street parking bays

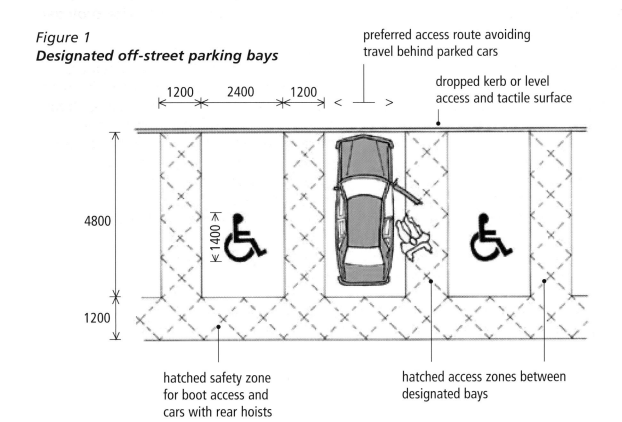

1200 2400 1200

preferred access route avoiding travel behind parked cars

dropped kerb or level access and tactile surface

4800

1400

1200

hatched safety zone for boot access and cars with rear hoists

hatched access zones between designated bays

Car parking

- The location of accessible bays should be clearly signposted from the car park entrance.

- Bays should be identified as provision for disabled drivers or passengers only.

- Information making it clear whether or not free parking is available to disabled motorists should be provided at the car park entrance.

- Bays should be as close as possible to (and in any case no more than 50m from) the principal entrance.

- In multi-storey car parks, designated spaces should ideally be at the same level as the principal (or alternative accessible) entrance or the main access route to and from the car park. Alternatively, a suitable passenger lift or ramp should be provided. Accessible bays are best grouped together so they are easier to find and to manage.

- Bays should be level (defined by AD M as predominantly level but with a maximum gradient along the direction of travel of 1:60), wide enough for car doors to be fully opened to allow disabled drivers and passengers to transfer to a wheelchair parked alongside and long enough to allow space for tail loading.

- All pedestrian routes within the car park should be level or with shallow gradients (see p 16 *Routes*).

- Kerbs between the parking area and routes to buildings should be dropped to give access to wheelchair users, with tactile warnings where appropriate (see *Guidance on the use of Tactile Paving Surfaces*).

- The car park surface should be smooth and even and free from loose stones, with undulations not exceeding 3mm under a 1m straight edge for materials such as tarmac or concrete.

- Where ticket machines are intended for use by disabled people, they should be located adjacent to designated parking bays and be accessible and convenient to use by someone in a wheelchair and someone of short stature (see *Figure 2*).

- See *Figure 3* for dimensions of on-street parking bays.

Figure 2
Accessible ticket-dispensing machines

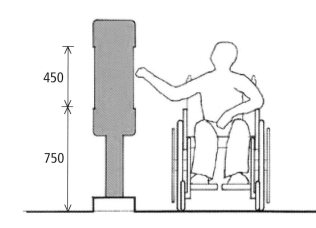
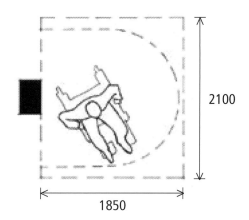

Setting-down points

People with mobility impairments who are passengers may need to be dropped off or picked up at a convenient point.

- Setting-down points should be clearly signposted and located on level ground as near to the principal entrance (or alternative accessible entrance) as possible.

- The surface of the footway should be level with the carriageway at the setting-down point, to allow convenient transfer to and from a wheelchair.

- For dimensions see *Figure 3*.

Figure 3
Example of on-street parking bay

Routes

Changes in level are difficult for many people to negotiate. As far as possible, access should be level or near level from the edge of the site or from designated accessible car parking spaces to the main entrance and/or other entrances used by disabled people and other principal routes around and between buildings.

- Where sections of the route have significant gradients (between 1:60 and 1:20), level landings should be provided for each 500mm rise.

- Where sections of the route have a gradient of 1:20 or steeper, design guidance on external ramps applies (see p 21).

- The cross-fall gradient of a path should not exceed 1:40 (except at dropped kerbs).

- There should be sufficient space for people, including wheelchair users, to approach the building and pass others travelling in the opposite direction. A width of 1800mm can accommodate any amount of non-vehicular traffic without the need for passing places; 1500mm in addition to passing places is acceptable on less busy routes; a width of 1200mm may be acceptable in exceptional circumstances on restricted sites (see *Figure 4* for path dimensions and *Figure 5* for passing places).

- Routes should be clearly signed, and may include landmarks for orientation. As well as providing visual clues they can also incorporate audible and olfactory clues such as fountains and fragrant planting.

Figure 4
Path dimensions

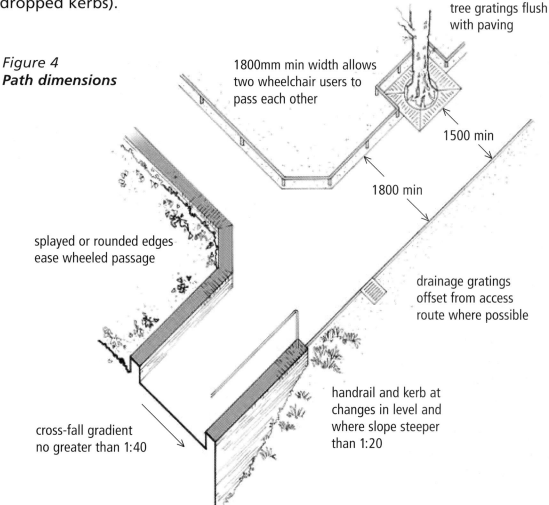

tree gratings flush with paving

1800mm min width allows two wheelchair users to pass each other

1500 min

1800 min

splayed or rounded edges ease wheeled passage

drainage gratings offset from access route where possible

cross-fall gradient no greater than 1:40

handrail and kerb at changes in level and where slope steeper than 1:20

Routes

Figure 5
Passing bays

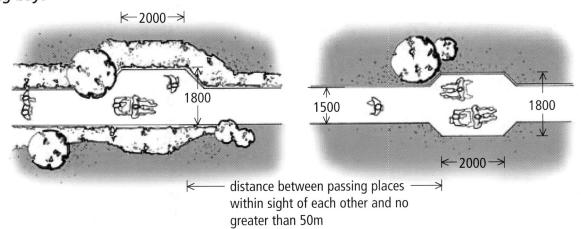

distance between passing places within sight of each other and no greater than 50m

- Pedestrian and vehicle routes should be clearly distinguished using texture and colour.

- Path edges should be defined (see *Figure 6*).

- Drainage channels should be flush with paving and designed to avoid trapping walking aids and wheels (see *Figure 7*).

- Surface materials should be firm, durable and slip-resistant in all weather (such as tarmac or York paving), with undulations not exceeding 3mm under a 1m straight edge for formless materials (such as tarmac or concrete), well laid and maintained.

- Surfaces such as sand, loose gravel, cobbles and terrazzo should be avoided.

- Surface materials can offer different sound qualities and textures as well as colour as an aid to locating the route within the environment.

- Where a variety of surface materials are used along access routes, materials should have similar frictional characteristics.

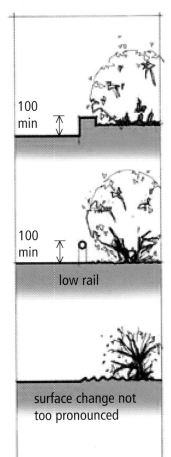

planting should be trimmed back to a height of at least 2.1m to avoid obstruction of the route

Figure 6
Path edges

Routes

- Joints between paving units should be detailed as follows:
  - filled joints, max difference in level 5mm
  - recessed joints, no deeper than 5mm and no wider than 10mm
  - unfilled joints, no wider than 5mm.

- Slip-resistant blister surface should be used to identify crossings with vehicular routes (see *Figures 8* and *10*). It is important to refer to *Guidance on the use of Tactile Paving Surfaces*.

- Planting can assist in defining routes or identifying hazards through scent and colour, but should not obstruct routes or prevent an overhead hazard.

- Signs should be carefully located, clear, non-reflective and logical (see p 54 *Wayfinding, information and signs*).

- Consider provision of seating at regular intervals, particularly on long or inclined routes (see p 50 *Seating*).

- Routes to main and/or alternative accessible entrances and potential hazards should be adequately lit.

- Low-level uplighters are not recommended because they cause glare.

- Lighting should not create pools of light and dark.

- Any objects that project more than 100mm onto an access route and have a lower edge more than 300mm from ground level should be protected (see *Figure 9*).

- Suitable protection may be by a kerb or other solid barrier that can be detected by a blind or partially sighted person using a cane and guarding between 900 and 1100mm from ground level.

  See also p 26 for guidance on hazard protection of entrance doors.

Figure 7
Drainage channels

circulation holes in gratings should be not more than 18mm diameter

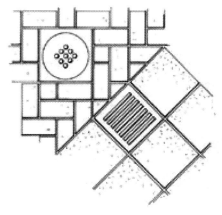

slots in gratings should be not more than 13mm wide and set at right angles to dominant line of travel

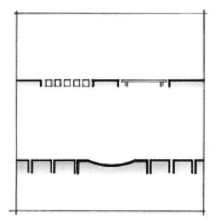

grids, gratings and covers flush with paving

shallow drainage channels to avoid trapping footrests etc

Figure 8
Blister tactile surface

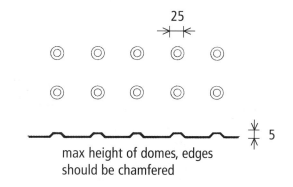

max height of domes, edges should be chamfered

Routes

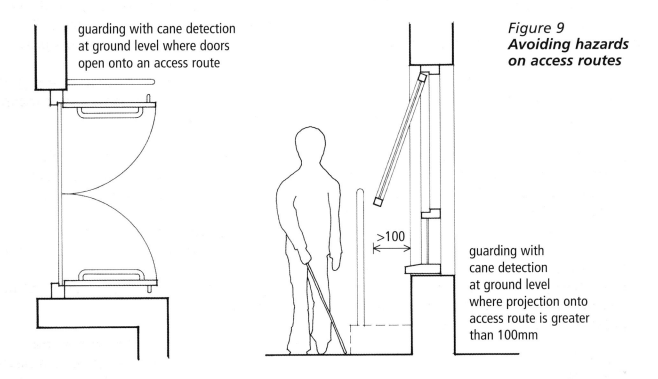

guarding with cane detection at ground level where doors open onto an access route

>100

guarding with cane detection at ground level where projection onto access route is greater than 100mm

Figure 9
Avoiding hazards on access routes

Figure 10
Tactile crossings

Dropped kerb

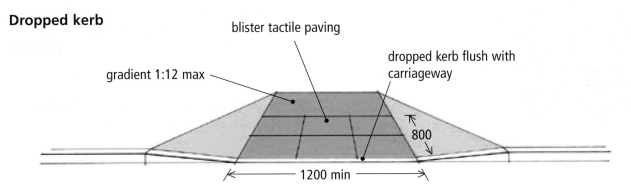

blister tactile paving

gradient 1:12 max

dropped kerb flush with carriageway

800

1200 min

Raised carriageway

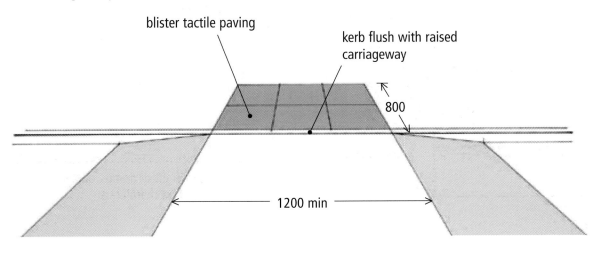

blister tactile paving

kerb flush with raised carriageway

800

1200 min

Street furniture

Careful positioning of street furniture provides easier access and reduces potential hazards, particularly for people with visual impairments.

- Clearly defined routes should be planned for pedestrians.

- Consider use of tonal contrast and/or textural changes in paving, logical grouping of street furniture, and effective lighting to define routes.

- Avoid where possible placing street furniture where it causes problems for people with sight impairments or obstructs the passage of wheelchair users (see *Figure 11*; see also p 54 *Wayfinding, information and signs*).

- If items of street furniture have to be located within access routes, they should be clearly identified, for example using contrasting colour and luminance with the background against which they will be seen. Avoid bench seats with open ends and sharp corners.

- The provision of appropriate seating is important, especially on long or sloping routes (see p 50 *Seating*).

- Avoid low headroom and safeguard building projections. Areas below stairs or ramps where there is less than 2100mm headroom above ground level should be protected by guarding and low-level cane detection, or a permanent barrier giving the same degree of protection. See also p 26 for guidance on protecting outward-opening doors.

- Bollards should be a minimum of 1000mm in height and tonally contrasted with background. Adjacent bollards should not be linked with a chain or rope.

- Free-standing posts or columns within access routes should incorporate a band of contrasting colour or luminance at 1500–1650mm. An additional band at 850–1000mm might also be considered.

- Cycle parking areas should be clear of pedestrian routes, and cycle stands should be clearly visible even when not in use.

Figure 11
Positioning of street furniture

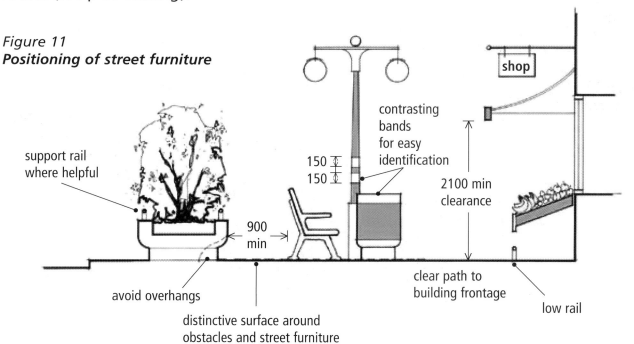

support rail where helpful

avoid overhangs

distinctive surface around obstacles and street furniture

900 min

150
150

contrasting bands for easy identification

2100 min clearance

clear path to building frontage

low rail

shop

External ramps

Where level access is not achievable, ramps enable wheelchair users and people with pushchairs to overcome level changes.

- Ramps should be accompanied by steps for ambulant disabled people where the rise of the ramp is greater than 300mm and by alternative means of access (a lift, for example) for wheelchair users if the total rise is greater than 2m.

- Ramped approaches should be clearly signed if not readily apparent.

- The permissible gradient of a ramp is dependent on the length between level landings (the 'going of the flight'). However, it should be noted that a route with a gradient of 1:20 over a significant distance can still be a potential barrier.

- Ramps should be as shallow as possible. The maximum permissible gradient is 1:12 (see *Figures 12*, *13* and *14*), with the occasional exception in the case of short, steeper ramps when refitting existing buildings.

- The total going of a ramp flight should not exceed 10m and the total rise should not exceed 500mm.

- Ramps should be at least 1500mm wide.

- In existing buildings where an extreme level change would require a long, circuitous ramp or where space is limited, a short-rise lift may be appropriate (see p 43 *Platform lifts*) either as an alternative or in addition to the ramp.

- Adequately large and unobstructed level landings at the bottom and top of the ramp and at any intermediate levels should be designed in accordance with *Figures 13* and *14*.

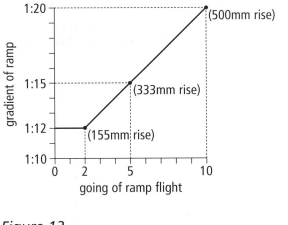

Figure 12
Ramp gradients

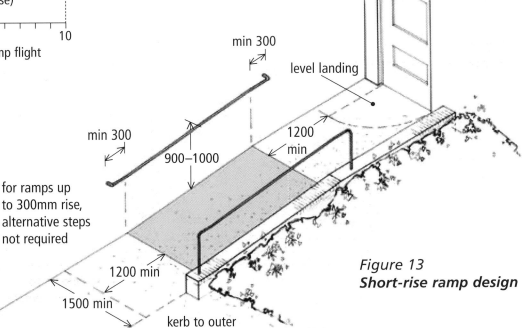

Figure 13
Short-rise ramp design

External ramps

- Intermediate landings at least 1800mm wide and 1800mm long should be provided as passing places when it is not possible for a wheelchair user to see from one end of the ramp to another or if the ramp has three flights or more.

- Level landings should have a maximum gradient of 1:60 along their length and a maximum cross-fall gradient of 1:40.

- Handrails, continuous to ramps and landings, should be provided to each side of the ramp set at appropriate heights and extending beyond the top and bottom of the flight (see *Figures 13* and *14*).

- A kerb at least 100mm high should be provided on the open side of any ramp or landing (in addition to any guarding required under Part K). It should contrast visually with the ramp and landing.

- Avoid patterning which simulates steps, such as applied or inserted slip-resistant strips.

- Surface materials should be slip-resistant when wet, firmly fixed and easy to maintain. The colour of the ramp surface should contrast visually with the landing surface. The frictional characteristics of the landing and ramp surfaces should be similar.

- It is not recommended to use corduroy tactile warnings to indicate ramps or lifts, as these are properly used to indicate the start of a flight of steps or stairs.

- Consideration should be given to adequate lighting.

Figure 14
Ramp design (with adjacent steps)

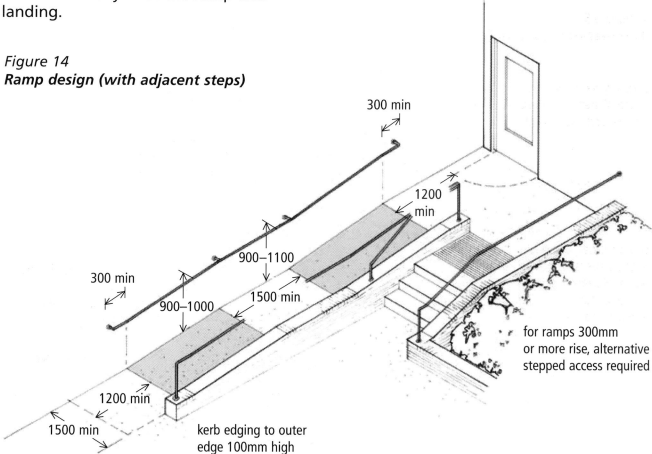

300 min

1200 min

900–1100

300 min

900–1000

1500 min

1200 min

1500 min

kerb edging to outer edge 100mm high

for ramps 300mm or more rise, alternative stepped access required

External steps

Steps should always be provided as an alternative to ramps steeper than 1:20, as they are preferred by some ambulant disabled people. Safety is an important consideration when designing and detailing flights of steps.

- For dimensions see *Figure 15*.

- Lighting can be located at the side of the flight, should be consistent along the full flight and adjoining landings, and should not cause anyone to negotiate the stairs in their own shadow.

- Straight flights are easier to negotiate than curved or dogleg flights.

- The unobstructed width of flights should be at least 1200mm.

- Handrails should be provided, however short the flight (see *Figure* 15 and p 25 *Handrails*).

- On wide flights of steps, handrails should be used to divide the flight into channels. AD M states that on flights of steps wider than 1800mm, handrails should be used to divide the flight into channels between 1000 and 1800mm, (but note anomaly here: taking into account the width of handrails, a flight needs to be at least 2050mm wide to be divided such that each channel is 1000mm wide).

- Level landings at least 1200mm long should be provided at the top and bottom of the flight of stairs, free of door swing across the landing (see *Figure* 15).

Figure 15
External stair dimensions

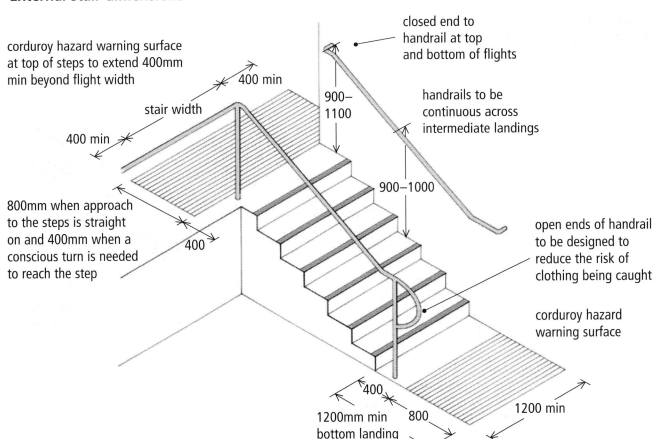

corduroy hazard warning surface at top of steps to extend 400mm min beyond flight width

400 min

stair width

400 min

800mm when approach to the steps is straight on and 400mm when a conscious turn is needed to reach the step

400

closed end to handrail at top and bottom of flights

900–1100

handrails to be continuous across intermediate landings

900–1000

open ends of handrail to be designed to reduce the risk of clothing being caught

corduroy hazard warning surface

400

1200mm min bottom landing

800

1200 min

External steps

- Surfaces should be slip-resistant.

- A 'corduroy' hazard warning surface of raised ribs set parallel to the step nosings should be provided at the top and bottom of each flight as a warning to people with sight impairments of the presence of a tripping hazard (*see Figure 16*).

- Corduroy surfaces should also be used at intermediate landings where there is access onto the landing other than from the steps themselves or on large intermediate landings where the handrails are not continuous.

- Nosings should be integral with the step and distinguishable in colour and tone (see *Figure 17*).

- Nosings should be used on the front face as well as on the top of each step so that they are visible when ascending and descending.

- A flight between landings should not contain more than 12 risers if the going is less than 350mm or 18 risers if the going is 350mm or more.

- The rise and going of each step should be consistent in a flight, between 150 and 170mm (with possible exceptions where adjacent to an existing building the riser may be greater than 170mm).

- Open risers should not be used.

- Spiral stairs, tapered treads and tapered risers are not recommended, as they are exceptionally difficult for many people.

- Avoid isolated single steps.

Figure 16
Corduroy tactile surface detail

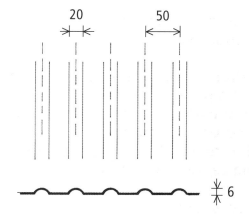

Figure 17
Nosings

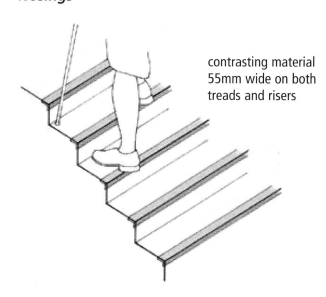

contrasting material 55mm wide on both treads and risers

Figure 18
Step profiles and number of risers

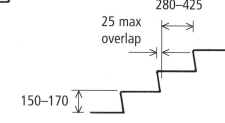

steps without projecting nosings are preferred

max 12 risers if going less than 350mm
max 18 risers if going 350mm or more

Handrails

People who have difficulty negotiating changes of level need the support of handrails. They should be provided in conjunction with changes in level, flights of ramps and steps.

- For heights of handrails see *Figures 13* and *14* (in relation to ramps), and *Figure 15* (in relation to steps).

- Handrails should be continuous across flights and landings.

- Consideration should be given to the provision of a second (lower) handrail set at 600mm on stairs, particularly in schools, for use by children and people of short stature.

- For handrail profiles and dimensions see *Figure 19*.

- Handrails should be easy to grip and provide good forearm support for people who are unable to grip. They should be configured with a positive end to reduce the risk of clothing being caught on the ends of rails.

- Surfaces such as hardwood or nylon-coated steel are recommended in preference to surface materials that are cold to the touch.

- The handrail should be easily distinguishable from its background, without being highly reflective.

Figure 19
Handrail profiles

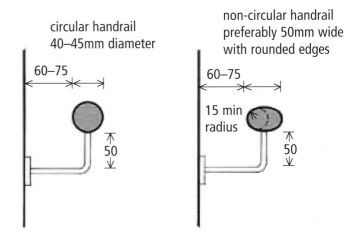

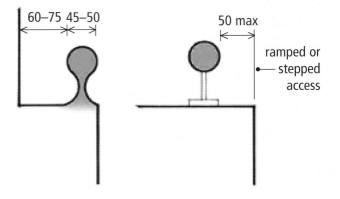

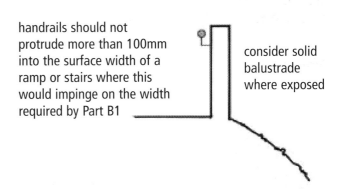

handrails should not protrude more than 100mm into the surface width of a ramp or stairs where this would impinge on the width required by Part B1

consider solid balustrade where exposed

Entrances

In new buildings, the principal entrance (or entrances) should be accessible. In existing buildings, where it is not possible for the main entrance (or entrances) to be accessible, an alternative entrance should be provided which is accessible for all potential users.

- Entrances to buildings should be placed in a logical relationship within the routes that serve them and be easily distinguishable from the façade.

- Alternative accessible entrances should be signposted both from the edge of the site and from the main entrance. Signs should incorporate the international access symbol.

- Clear signs indicating the entrance should be provided, visible from all approaches to the building. Signs hanging perpendicular to the building facade can be useful.

- The area immediately in front of the accessible entrance (at least 1500mm x 1500mm) should be level and have a surface which does not impede wheelchairs. Structural supports should be clearly identifiable so that they do not present a hazard for visually impaired people.

- Canopies over entrances should be considered as protection from bad weather, particularly at entrances with manual doors or entry systems.

- Outward-opening doors should be protected or recessed (see *Figure 20*).

- The approach to door entry controls should be clear of obstructions and away from any projecting columns or return walls.

Figure 20
Outward-opening doors

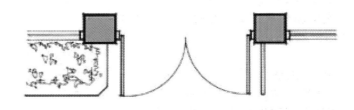

- Door entry systems should be accessible to people with hearing impairments and people who cannot speak. Visual contact could be made possible either through a window or via an entryphone with a visual display.

- Security systems such as swipe cards should be detailed to allow use by people with sensory or mobility impairments.

- Turnstiles are difficult for most people with mobility impairments. If used, there should be at least one alternative access gate.

- See *Figure 23* for unobstructed space on the pull side of the door between the leading edge of the door and any return wall.

- Thresholds should be flush wherever possible. A maximum change in level of 15mm is permissible if clearly visible and floor finishes are graded to provide a flush junction.

Entrances

Entrances

- Any upstands greater than 5mm should be chamfered or pencil-rounded.

- Internal floor surfaces adjacent to thresholds should be easy for wheelchair passage. Any changes in floor materials should not create a potential trip hazard.

- A firm and flush entrance mat should be provided extending a minimum 1500mm into the building (see p 39 *Surfaces*). Coir matting should be avoided.

  See also p 29 *Entrance doors* for widths of doors and detailed guidance on entrance door design.

Lobbies
- Lobbies should be sized to allow wheelchair users and an accompanying helper to move clear of the first door before negotiating the second. See *Figure 22* for various acceptable lobby configurations.

- Where lobbies have automatic sliding doors or reduced swing doors, the length of the lobby may be reduced as less space is needed for wheelchair manoeuvre.

- Immediately after entering there should be a transition zone where lighting is used to aid people with visual impairments to adjust to changes in light levels from the exterior to the interior environment.

- Signs should be obvious and clear, indicating where visitors should go to find the reception area, information point, lifts, stairs or WCs.

- Glazing within the lobby should not create distracting reflections.

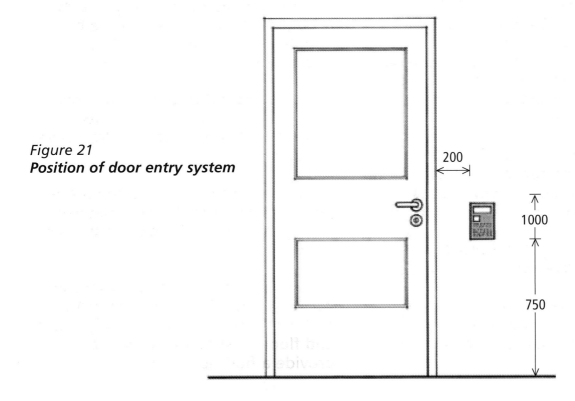

Figure 21
Position of door entry system

200

1000

750

Entrances

Figure 22
Entrance lobbies

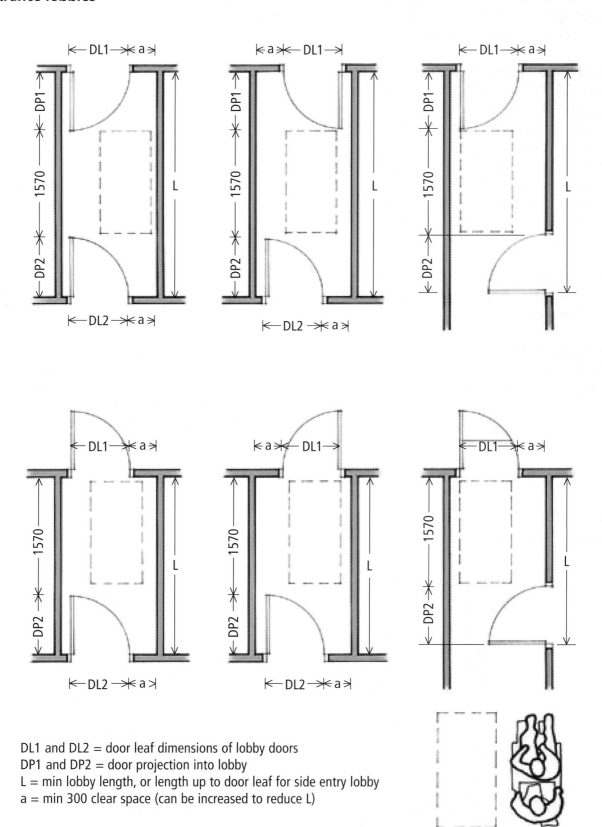

DL1 and DL2 = door leaf dimensions of lobby doors
DP1 and DP2 = door projection into lobby
L = min lobby length, or length up to door leaf for side entry lobby
a = min 300 clear space (can be increased to reduce L)

1570mm-long space represents
area for wheelchair user and assistant

Entrance doors

Doors to the principal or alternative entrance should be accessible to all, including wheelchair users and people with limited manual dexterity.

- The minimum effective clear width (see *Figure 23*) of external doors should be 1000mm in new buildings and 775mm in existing buildings (although 1000mm is preferred). Effective clear width should be measured from the face of the door when open to the opposite frame or doorstop (but note that protruding door furniture may reduce usable opening).

- Doors and/or door frames should be clearly identified by tonally contrasting with the wall.

- Doors and side panels wider than 450mm should normally have vision panels (see *Figure 24*).

Figure 23
Effective clear width of doors

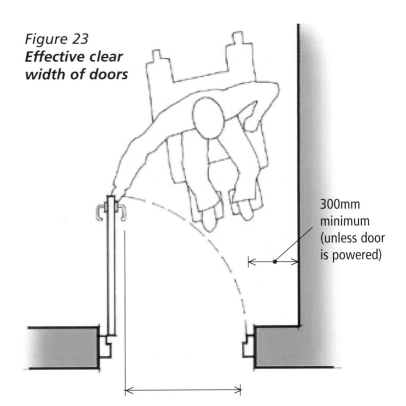

300mm minimum (unless door is powered)

effective clear width – measured from the face of the door when open to the opposite frame or doorstop taking into account door handle or any other protruding door furniture

Figure 24
Visibility requirements

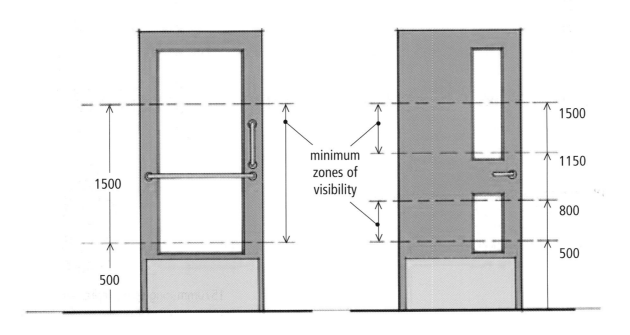

1500

500

1500

1150

800

500

minimum zones of visibility

Entrance doors

- Substantially glazed doors or side panels should bear markings for safety and visibility (see *Figure 25*). It is recommended that markings are two-tone to be visible against a variety of backgrounds and lighting conditions. Consideration could be given to using a company logo, sign or decorative feature.

- Glazed entrance doors, where adjacent to or forming part of a glazed screen, should be clearly differentiated by highly contrasting strips at the top and on both sides.

- Fully glazed, frameless entrance doors are not recommended. If used, and where capable of being held open, they should be protected by guarding to prevent the leading edge constituting a hazard.

- For double doors, it is preferred that both are kept in regular use. If one is locked, clearly identify the leaf in regular use.

Manually operated doors

- Manually operated doors, including those with self-closing devices, are difficult for many people to open. Particularly where doors are heavy, consideration should be given to providing automatic opening (see p 32 *Powered doors*) or closers linked to fire alarm installations or low-energy swing-door operators.

- The opening force should be as low as reasonably practicable. AD M recommends that the opening force at the leading edge of the door should not be greater than 20 newtons. See also p 61 *Building management checklist*.

- Where self-closing devices are fitted to manually operated doors, these should be slow in operation and regularly maintained.

- Door furniture should be clearly distinguishable from the door using tonal contrast and be designed to be easily reached and gripped.

Figure 25
Markings for safety and visibility

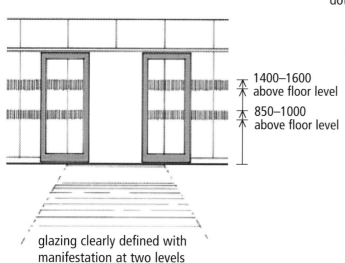

1400–1600 above floor level

850–1000 above floor level

glazing clearly defined with manifestation at two levels

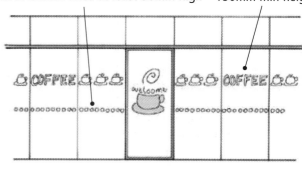

decorative feature such as repeated dots or broken lines at least 50mm high

decorative logo 150mm min height

high-contrast strips to top, bottom and both sides of glazed door to clearly differentiate from glazed screen

Entrance doors

- Door handles should be selected for ease of grip by people with poor manual dexterity and, where fitted with a latch, should be operable with one hand using a closed fist, such as a lever action handle (see *Figure 26* and for positioning *Figure 27*).

- Full-height door pulls can be useful but may restrict effective clear width, as may substantial weather boards. Additional opening width should be provided to accommodate these.

Figure 26
Door handle details

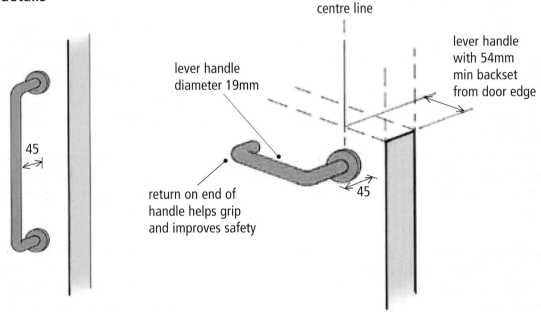

centre line

lever handle with 54mm min backset from door edge

lever handle diameter 19mm

45

45

return on end of handle helps grip and improves safety

Figure 27
Height of door handles

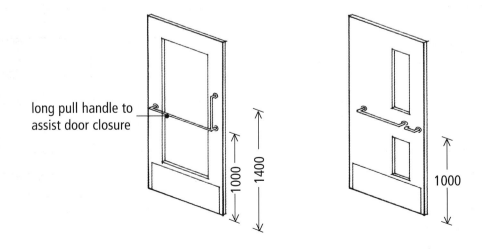

long pull handle to assist door closure

1000

1400

1000

Entrance doors

Powered doors

Powered door-opening and closing systems are generally recommended in preference to non-powered, manually operated doors.

- Automatic sliding doors, activated by a motion sensor or other trigger, generally offer very good access.

- Automatic doors should open early enough and stay open long enough to allow safe entry and exit, particularly for people who move slowly. Ensure that the sensor and delay mechanism are adjustable.

- They should incorporate a safety stop that is activated if the doors start to close when a person is passing through them and revert to manual control or failsafe in the open position in the event of a power failure.

- With doors that swing towards the user both visual and audible warnings are recommended. When open, they should not project into any adjacent access route.

- Manual controls – push pads, card swipes, proximity readers or coded entry – for powered doors should be located between 750 and 1000mm above floor level and set back 1400mm from the leading edge of the door (so that the user does not have to move to avoid contact with the door as it opens). They should be clearly distinguishable from the background.

- Revolving doors of whatever size are not considered accessible. Ambulant disabled people, older people, those with sight impairments and guide dogs may not have the confidence to negotiate them. If used they should be supplemented with a fully operational swing door.

Entrance foyers

Well-designed entrance foyers provide a transition from the outside to the inside, and can help orientate people once inside the building.

- Clear view in from outside is helpful.

- The area should be well lit, with plenty of circulation space. Routes to reception counters, lifts, stairs and WCs should be easily visible, clearly defined and unobstructed.

- The reception point should be located away from the principal entrance (while still providing a view of it) to reduce impact of external noise. Where sliding glass windows are installed they should be fully openable to allow for audible conversation.

- At reception, both the receptionist's face and visitors' faces should be clearly visible and well lit to allow lip reading.

See *Figure 28* and also guidance on *Counters and service desks,* p 51 and *Induction loops,* p 59.

Figure 28
Entrance foyers

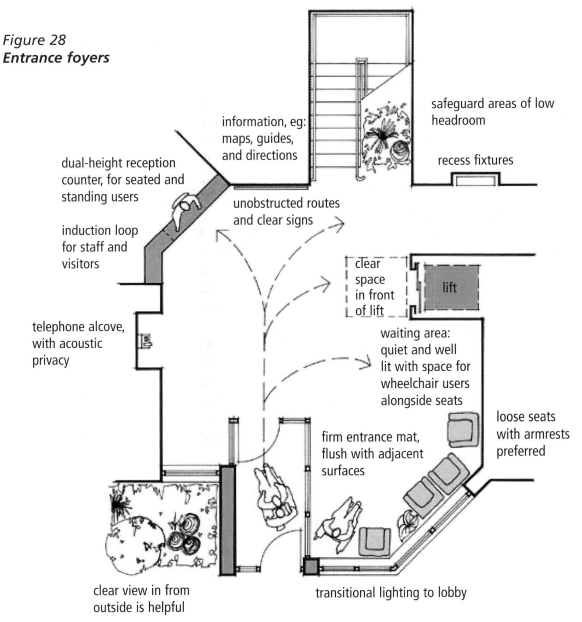

information, eg: maps, guides, and directions

safeguard areas of low headroom

recess fixtures

dual-height reception counter, for seated and standing users

induction loop for staff and visitors

unobstructed routes and clear signs

clear space in front of lift

lift

telephone alcove, with acoustic privacy

waiting area: quiet and well lit with space for wheelchair users alongside seats

loose seats with armrests preferred

firm entrance mat, flush with adjacent surfaces

clear view in from outside is helpful

transitional lighting to lobby

clearly identifiable entrance

Circulation

Designing open-plan spaces – for example in offices, restaurants, exhibition spaces, entrance foyers and shopping centres – reduces the need for internal doors, which create potential barriers to easy movement around a building.

- A minimum clear circulation width of 1200mm should be provided, and maintained when furniture layouts are altered.

- For large open-plan areas, consider defining routes with contrasting floor finishes and textures.

- Ensure adequate tonal contrast in colour schemes.

- Lighting systems can be used to help define circulation routes in open-plan spaces.

Corridors

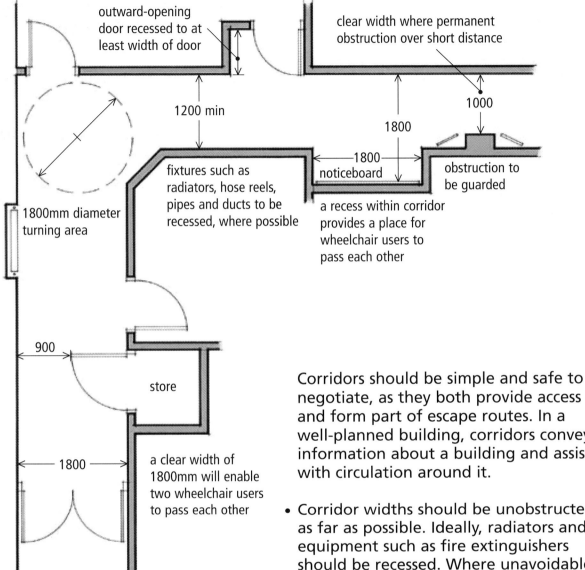

outward-opening door recessed to at least width of door

clear width where permanent obstruction over short distance

1200 min

1000

1800

1800
noticeboard

fixtures such as radiators, hose reels, pipes and ducts to be recessed, where possible

obstruction to be guarded

a recess within corridor provides a place for wheelchair users to pass each other

1800mm diameter turning area

900

store

1800

a clear width of 1800mm will enable two wheelchair users to pass each other

Figure 29
Corridor dimensions

Corridors should be simple and safe to negotiate, as they both provide access and form part of escape routes. In a well-planned building, corridors convey information about a building and assist with circulation around it.

- Corridor widths should be unobstructed as far as possible. Ideally, radiators and equipment such as fire extinguishers should be recessed. Where unavoidable, there should be a means of directing people around them, such as a visually contrasting guardrail.

- Doors that open outwards into a corridor that is in regular use should be recessed. Exceptions may be outward-opening doors to unisex wheelchair-accessible WCs (so long as the corridor is at least 1800mm wide and the door closes in the direction of emergency escape) and doors to minor utility facilities such as small store rooms and locked duct cupboards.

Corridors

- Along a major access route or an escape route, if there is a series of double doors with one leaf wider than the other, the wider leaf should be on the same side over the length of the corridor.

- Avoid glazing at ends of corridors, since this can cause visual confusion.

- Where corridor widths in existing buildings are narrow, wider doors should be considered.

- Floors within a corridor should be level (up to a gradient of 1:60) wherever possible. Where a section of a corridor has a gradient between 1:60 and 1:20 in the direction of travel, the sloped surface should be clearly differentiated and there should be a level rest area at least 1500mm long for every 500mm rise in level.

- Any sections within a corridor steeper than 1:20 should be designed as an internal ramp (see p 40).

- Where a section of corridor is divided (for example between a level and a sloping section) the exposed edge should be clearly identified by visual contrast and, where necessary, protected by guarding.

- Avoid colour schemes with little tonal contrast, or patterned surfaces on floors which may be mistaken for steps or changes in level. Doors, floors, walls and ceilings should be defined using tonal contrast.

- Lighting should be located where it does not create glare or silhouettes.

- Wall and floor surfaces should be chosen to minimise light reflection and sound reverberation, which can be confusing for people with sensory impairments.

- Consider also guarding of projecting hazards and avoid glazing that creates distracting reflections (see p 39 *Surfaces*).

For various acceptable layouts of internal lobbies, see *Figure 22*.

Internal doors

The main consideration regarding a door is whether it is actually necessary or whether it could be 'designed out'. If the door is required and is on a main circulation route or provides access to a key facility or service, ease of use is a priority.

- The minimum effective clear width (see *Figure 23*) of internal doors varies according to the type of door, angle of approach and width of access routes (see table below). Effective clear width should be measured from the face of the door when open to the opposite frame or doorstop (but note that protruding door furniture may reduce usable opening).

- In existing buildings where it is not possible to achieve 800mm, internal doors should provide a minimum 750mm effective clear width (or 775mm as against 825mm for doors at right angles to corridors narrower than 1200mm).

- Doors and/or door frames should be clearly identified by tonally contrasting with the wall.

- The surface of the leading edge of any door that is not self-closing, or is likely to be held open, should contrast visually with the other door surfaces and its surroundings.

- Doors (and side panels wider than 450mm) should normally have vision panels (see *Figure 24*).

- Substantially glazed doors or side panels should bear markings for safety and visibility (see *Figure 25*). It is recommended that markings are two-tone to be visible against a variety of backgrounds and lighting conditions. Consideration could be given to using a company logo, sign or decorative feature.

- For double doors, the leaf in regular use should be clearly identified. The minimum required effective clear width should be provided through at least one leaf.

- Door furniture should be clearly distinguishable from the door using tonal contrast and be designed to be easily reached and gripped.

- Door handles should be selected for ease of grip by people with limited manual dexterity and operable with one

Minimum effective clear widths of internal doors as recommended in AD M		
Direction and width of approach	New buildings (mm)	Existing buildings (mm)
Straight on (without a turn or oblique approach)	800	750
At right angles to an access route at least 1500mm wide	800	750
At right angles to an access route at least 1200mm wide	825	775

Internal doors

hand using a closed fist, such as a lever action (see *Figure 26* and for positioning *Figure 27*).

- Full-height door pulls can be useful but may restrict effective clear width, as may substantial weather boards. Additional opening width should be provided to accommodate these.

- Particularly where doors are heavy, consideration should be given to providing automatic opening, electromagnetic catches which hold doors open or closers linked to fire alarm installations or low-energy swing-door operators. Any low-energy, powered swing door systems should be capable of being operated in manual mode, powered mode or power-assisted mode.

- Where doors are opened manually, the opening force should be as low as reasonably practicable. AD M recommends that the opening force at the leading edge of the door should not be greater than 20 newtons. See also p 61 *Building management checklist.*

Surfaces

The selection of floor surfaces is of considerable importance to all building users. Considered choice of surfaces can aid orientation, acoustic conditions, ease of passage for wheelchairs and buggies, and safety.

General

- Hard surfaces can cause sound reverberation and increased background noise levels, which can cause difficulties for people with hearing impairments. A mixture of hard and soft surfaces should be used.

- A combination of colour, tonal and textural contrast helps people with sight impairments to distinguish between surfaces and objects placed upon them, such as switches on walls and litter bins on floors.

- Tonal contrast is more important than colour contrast. Some colours which appear to be different can be tonally similar under certain lighting conditions or for people who have difficulty distinguishing colours.

- Textured surfaces are important in providing information to people with little or no sight.

Floors

- Floor surfaces should be firm and non-directional to allow easy passage for wheelchair users.

- Carpets should be of shallow dense pile. Avoid coir matting, deep pile or excessively grooved carpet.

- Junctions between different flooring materials should be carefully detailed so as not to create an obstacle to wheelchair users or a tripping hazard for people with mobility or visual impairment.

- Textured floors can warn of hazards or impart directional information.

- Floor surfaces should be slip-resistant. This is of particular importance to people who use walking aids such as sticks or crutches, and to older people. See BS 8300, Annex C: *Slip potential characteristics of tread and floor finishes.*

- Floor areas that may become wet – just inside the entrance to covered shopping malls for example – should not be of a type that becomes slippery. Entrance mats should be considered.

- Glossy floors cause reflection and glare, which can create difficulties for people with visual impairments. They can also give the illusion of being wet and slippery even if they are not, which may inhibit people with mobility impairments.

- Avoid types of floors that become hazardous when recently washed.

- Bright, boldly patterned flooring should be avoided as it can create a confusing impression for people with impaired sight.

Walls

- Wall coverings should not be busy or distracting. This can cause difficulties for wayfinding or those needing to lip read.

- Glossy walls cause reflection and glare, which can create difficulties for people with visual impairments.

- Textured walls (of fine rather than rough grain) can alert people to the presence of facilities such as WCs or lifts where a key to the understanding of this system has been given in advance.

Internal stairs, ramps and handrails

Stairs and ramps should be designed for ease of use and safety for all building users. Guidance is broadly similar to that for external steps and ramps.

Stairs

- Follow guidance on *External steps*, p 23 and *Figure 15*, except that hazard warnings are not required at the top and bottom landings (although tactile warnings may be incorporated into handrails).

- Flights should contain not more than 12 risers between landings or, exceptionally, up to 16 risers in small buildings where space is restricted.

- The rise of steps should be between 150 and 170mm, except in existing buildings with space constraints, where a higher rise may be acceptable.

- Spiral stairs and tapered treads are not recommended.

- Open risers should not be used.

- Avoid single steps.

Ramps

- Follow guidance on *External ramps*, p 21 and *Figures 13* and *14*.

- Where the change in level is more than 300mm, two or more clearly signposted steps should be provided in addition to the ramp; where the change in level is not more than 300mm, a ramp should be provided instead of a single step.

Handrails

- Follow guidance as for *Handrails*, p 25.

- Height of handrails should be 900–1000mm above pitch line and 900–1100mm at landings.

Passenger lifts

For people who cannot use stairs, a passenger lift is the preferred form of access from one storey to another for all buildings.

- *Figure 30* shows the minimum lift car dimensions to accommodate a wheelchair user and an accompanying person. This size does not allow a wheelchair user to turn around inside the lift. Therefore, a mirror (bottom edge 900mm from the floor) should be provided in the lift car to enable a wheelchair user to see which level the lift has reached.

- Larger-size lifts are preferred where possible and may in fact be required depending on the building type and use. For example, a lift compartment 2000mm wide by 1400mm deep will accommodate most types of wheelchair together with several other standing passengers.

- Fold-down or perch seats in larger lifts could be considered.

- Lifts should be served by landings large enough for wheelchair users to turn to reverse into the lift (see *Figure 30*).

- The call panel should be easily distinguishable from its background.

- Lift buttons should be clearly distinguishable. 'Lift coming' indication should be clear from any position

Figure 30
Lift car dimensions

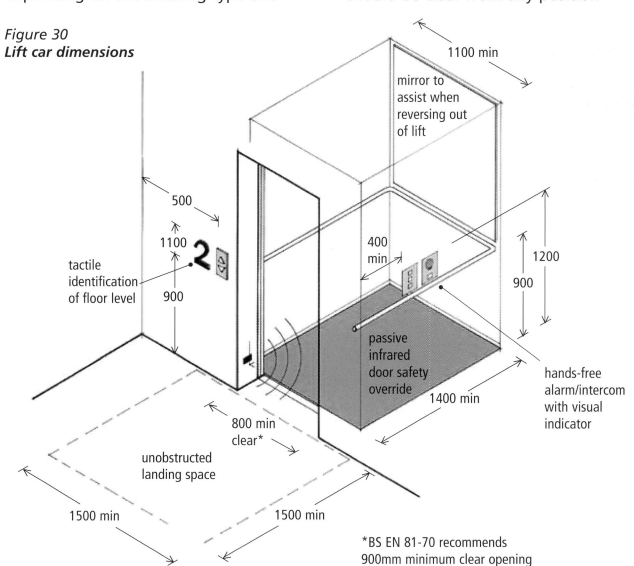

500

1100

tactile identification of floor level

900

1100 min

mirror to assist when reversing out of lift

400 min

1200

900

passive infrared door safety override

1400 min

hands-free alarm/intercom with visual indicator

800 min clear*

unobstructed landing space

1500 min

1500 min

*BS EN 81-70 recommends 900mm minimum clear opening

Passenger lifts

within the lift lobby. Where there is more than one lift, ensure people with mobility impairments have time to get to the relevant lift.

- The floor area outside the lift and lift car doors should be visually distinguishable from the adjoining walls.

- Provide visual and tactile indication of floor level adjacent to call buttons and opposite lift doors.

- An embossed sign indicating the number of the floor should be provided on each lift landing on the wall opposite the lift. The sign should be visually contrasting with its background.

- Power-operated horizontal sliding doors should provide an effective clear width of at least 800mm according to AD M. However, BS EN 81-70:2003 recommends a minimum of 900mm, which is more suitable for wheelchairs and double buggies.

- Lift doors should remain open for five seconds, providing an adequate time for entry. Door reactivating devices which rely on infrared or photo eye systems are necessary to ensure no one can get trapped in the doors.

- Control panels should be located on a side wall, and preferably on both side walls of the lift car, at a height that can be easily reached by someone in a wheelchair (see *Figure 30*). Raised and well-contrasted numbers on buttons help people with sight impairments. Braille can also be used, although many visually impaired people do not read Braille.

- Audible announcements and visual displays are recommended internally and externally on all lifts to indicate floor reached or inform that the doors are open.

- Emergency telephones in lifts should be easy to use (for example, intercom and push-button activation rather than hand-held) and contain inductive couplers so that hearing aid users can make use of them.

- Alarm buttons in lifts should be fitted with a visual acknowledgement that the alarm bell has sounded for lift users unable to hear it.

- The floor of the lift car should have frictional qualities similar to or higher than the floor area outside the lift.

- Lighting and surfaces within the lift car should minimise glare, reflection, confusing shadows and pools of light and dark. Lights adjacent to control panels are not recommended because they could make it difficult for people to read controls.

- Lifts that are designated for use in emergency to evacuate people should be fitted with an independent power supply.

- Areas of glass should be identifiable by people with impaired vision.

- Acceleration and deceleration rates should be set to avoid jolting.

- Passenger lifts should conform to the requirements of the Lift Regulations 1997 (SI 1997/831) and, if used to evacuate disabled people in an emergency, to the relevant recommendations of BS 5588-8.

Platform lifts

While not ideal, platform lifts may be acceptable to overcome changes in level where passenger lifts or ramps are not possible due to space constraints. Disadvantages include slow travel speed and the need for application of continuous pressure on controls, which may be difficult for some people.

- Platform lifts should be located adjacent to the stair with which they are associated.

- They should be designed for independent use with clearly visible controls set at a suitable height for wheelchair users, clear instructions for use and fitted with an emergency alarm.

- Platforms need to be large enough to accommodate a range of users. A larger platform may be required for powered wheelchairs or accompanied wheelchair users (see *Figure 31* for dimensions).

- Where the vertical travel distance exceeds 2m and/or the lift penetrates a floor, there should be a liftway enclosure (see *Figure 32*).

- Lift controls should be located between 800 and 1100mm from the floor of the lifting platform and at least 400mm from any return wall.

- Acceleration and deceleration rates should be set to avoid jolting.

- Platform lifts should conform to the requirements of the Supply of Machinery (Safety) Regulations 1992, SI 1992/3073.

See also section on *Passenger lifts,* p 41, and *Figure 30* for guidance on landing controls, distinguishing doors from walls, audible and visual announcements and identifying areas of glass, and BS 6440: 1999 *Powered lifting platforms for use by disabled persons – Code of practice.*

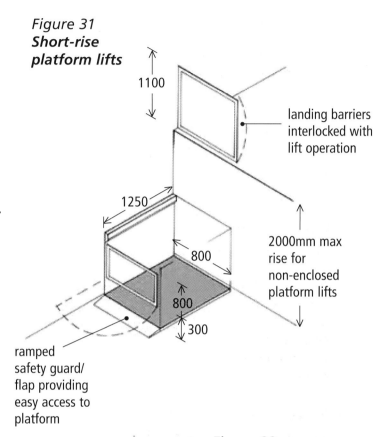

Figure 31
Short-rise platform lifts

1100

landing barriers interlocked with lift operation

1250

800

2000mm max rise for non-enclosed platform lifts

800

300

ramped safety guard/ flap providing easy access to platform

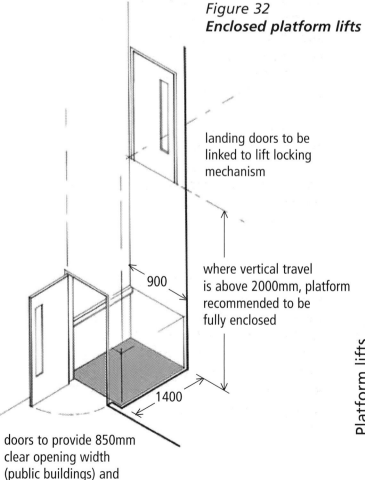

Figure 32
Enclosed platform lifts

landing doors to be linked to lift locking mechanism

900

where vertical travel is above 2000mm, platform recommended to be fully enclosed

1400

doors to provide 850mm clear opening width (public buildings) and vision panel

Platform lifts

Wheelchair platform stairlifts

Wheelchair platform stairlifts may – in exceptional circumstances – be suitable in adapting existing buildings where it is not feasible to install a passenger lift or vertical-rise platform lift. They are not appropriate in new buildings. Although designed to be operated independently, they are only suitable where users can be instructed in their safe use and under management supervision. Like vertical-rise platform lifts, disadvantages include slow travel speed and the need for application of continuous pressure on controls, which may be difficult for some people.

- Minimum dimensions are 800mm x 1250mm (see *Figure 33*).

- Ensure that the stairlift has controls that are designed to prevent unauthorised use and an alarm. A means of communication with building staff is recommended should assistance be required.

- In a building with a single stairway, ensure that the required clear flight width for means of escape is maintained, including when the lift platform is folded up and parked. Consult with fire officer before installation.

- Wheelchair platform stairlifts should conform to the requirements of the Supply of Machinery (Safety) Regulations 1992, SI 1992/3073.

Figure 33
Wheelchair platform stairlifts

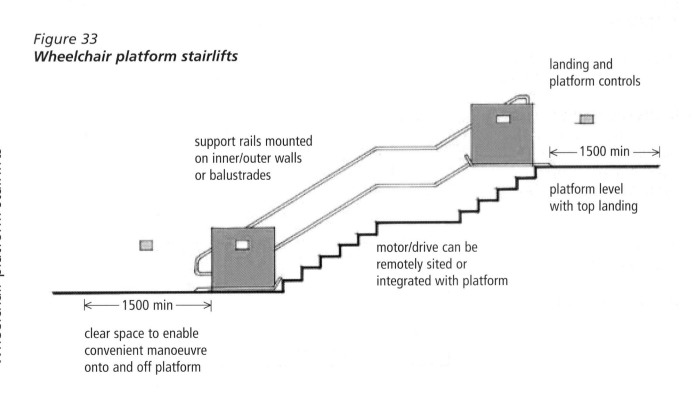

landing and platform controls

support rails mounted on inner/outer walls or balustrades

1500 min

platform level with top landing

motor/drive can be remotely sited or integrated with platform

1500 min

clear space to enable convenient manoeuvre onto and off platform

Wheelchair platform stairlifts

WCs

Suitable and easily identifiable sanitary accommodation should be provided for all building users. This will involve combinations of general provision, accommodation for ambulant disabled people and others who need more space, and wheelchair users. Appropriate provision will vary according to type and size of building and use patterns. Issues relating to provision, design and use of WCs are covered in more detail in CAE/RIBA Enterprises' *Good Loo Design Guide*.

General guidance

- In general, there should be at least as many WCs for women as there are urinals for men, and in some building types, such as large retail buildings, at least twice as many.

- Doors to WC cubicles and wheelchair-accessible unisex compartments should, preferably, open out. If they open in, they should not encroach unduly on usable space (see *Figure 34*). Reduced-swing doors could be used where space outside is restricted.

- Doors, when open, should not obstruct emergency escape routes.

- Doors should be fitted with light-action privacy bolts that can be operated by people with limited dexterity. If self-closing, they should be openable using a force of no more than 20 newtons.

- Emergency release mechanisms which can be operated from the outside should be fitted to doors.

- For guidance on door handles and other ironmongery, see p 37 *Internal doors*. Locks to cubicles should be operable by people with limited dexterity.

- Shiny ceramic tiles and floors should be avoided. They cause reflection and glare, which may be visually confusing.

- Slip-resistant flooring materials should be used.

- Fixtures and fittings within the WC compartment should be clearly visible using tonal contrast.

- The recommended height from the floor to the top of the WC seat is 480mm for WCs used by adults.

- Any washbasin taps should be controlled by a lever-operated, thermostatic mixer that delivers water at a temperature not exceeding 41°C.

- Any heat emitters should be either screened or have their exposed surfaces maintained at less than 43°C.

- Light switches with large push pads should be used in preference to pull cords.

Figure 34
Standard WC compartment with inward-opening door

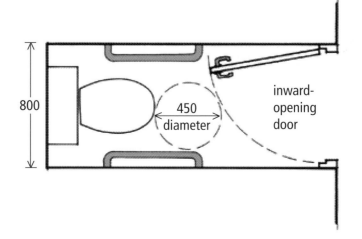

800

450 diameter

inward-opening door

WCs

- Emergency assistance alarm systems linked to a staffed area of the building should be provided. They should have visual and audible indicators to confirm that an emergency call has been received, a reset control reachable from the WC or from a wheelchair, and a signal that is different from the fire alarm.

- Any fire alarms should emit a visual and audible warning to occupants of WCs.

- Any wheelchair-accessible WC should have at least one washbasin with its rim set between 720 and 740mm above the floor.

- Paper dispensers should be designed for single-hand operation.

- Male wheelchair-accessible WCs should have at least one urinal with its rim set at 380mm above the floor, with two 600mm-long vertical grabrails positioned at either side of the urinal (with centre lines at 1100mm).

- Consider privacy screens for urinals where grabrails are not provided.

- A low-level urinal and washbasin for children and people of short stature in male WCs are recommended.

For more detail on all aspects of the design of accessible WCs, see the *Good Loo Design Guide* and BS 8300.

WC layout for ambulant disabled people

- At least one cubicle per range of WC compartments within separate-sex accommodation should be provided which is suitable for ambulant disabled people (see *Figure 35*).

- Ensure that the grabrails protrude no more than approximately 90mm so as not to restrict space within the cubicle. Ensure adequate knuckle space behind rails.

- Doors should open outwards wherever possible, and be fitted with a horizontal closing bar on the inside face. If a door opens inwards, the 750mm-long activity space should be maintained (see *Figure 35*). The door should be designed so that it can be opened outwards in an emergency.

- WC pans should conform to BS 5503-3 or BS 5504-4 so that they are able to accommodate a variable-height seat riser.

- Provide a shelf if space permits.

- Provide a coat hook at 1200–1400mm high.

- Where there are four or more WC cubicles in separate-sex accommodation, one of these should be 1200mm wide for use by people who need extra space. Consideration should be given to installing a fold-down table for baby changing.

- Where a larger separate-sex WC can be accessed by wheelchair users, it should be possible for them to use both a urinal, where appropriate, and a washbasin at a lower height than is provided for other users.

For guidance on layout and dimensions of wheelchair-accessible compartments within single-sex accommodation, see *The unisex accessible corner WC* below and *Figure 36, p 49*.

The unisex accessible corner WC

- Wheelchair users use WCs in a variety of ways. This may be independently or with assistance. Transfer to the WC from a wheelchair could be from the

WCs

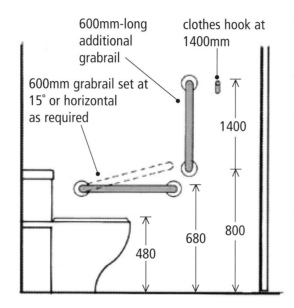

Figure 35
WC layout for ambulant disabled people

600mm-long additional grabrail

clothes hook at 1400mm

600mm grabrail set at 15° or horizontal as required

1400

1400

800

680

480

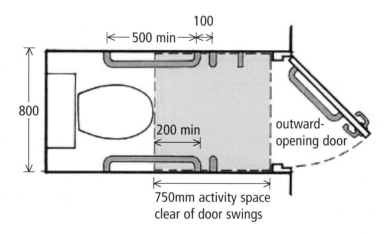

100

|←— 500 min —→|

800

200 min

outward-opening door

750mm activity space clear of door swings

front, side or at an angle. Some may transfer backwards with assistance by removing the wheelchair back support.

- At least one accessible unisex WC (see *Figure 36*) should be provided at each location where sanitary accommodation is provided for use by customers, visitors or employees.

- The recommended number and location of wheelchair-accessible WCs depends on the size and use of the building. A wheelchair user should not have to travel more 40m on one level (except in circumstances where the access route is completely free of obstructions such as doors which need to be opened) or more than 40m total horizontal distance

using a passenger lift to get to the next storey up or down.

- Where there is space for only one WC in a building, it should be a unisex accessible WC but wider (2000mm) than the standard wheelchair-accessible compartment (1500mm) to accommodate a standing-height washbasin in addition to the finger-rinse basin.

- One compartment should be located as close as possible to the entrance and/or waiting area.

- They should be located on direct, accessible routes that are free from obstruction and such that they do not compromise the privacy of users.

WCs

- If located in a similar position on each floor of a multi-storey building, right-handed and left-handed transfer should be provided on alternate floors.

- Where more than one unisex WC is available in single-storey buildings, a choice of layouts suitable for right-hand and left-hand transfer should be provided.

- Where the layouts are handed, the door configuration should be handed accordingly.

- Combining baby-changing facilities within AD M layout WC compartments which are likely to be in frequent use should be avoided.

- The unisex accessible corner WC can accommodate a variety of methods of transfer and allows most users to wash and dry their hands while seated on the WC before transferring back to their chair (see *Figure 36*).

- Overall dimensions shown in *Figure 36* are minimum and could be increased to advantage.

- Doors should open outwards wherever possible, and be fitted with a horizontal closing bar on the inside face. Where inward-opening doors are unavoidable, additional space is required, and it should be possible to open the door outwards in an emergency.

- The dimensions relating WC fitting to basin and associated fittings and equipment, and to wheelchair manoeuvring space, are critical for independent use.

- The horizontal rail/backrest to the rear of the WC should be padded if there is no WC lid to rest against. A backrest may not be required so long as the cistern is low-level and comfortable to lean against.

- WC pans should conform to BS 5503-3 or BS 5504-4 so that they are able to accommodate a variable-height seat riser.

- The flush should be easy to operate and mounted on the transfer side of the cistern within easy reach. A lever-type flush is recommended.

- Plastic-coated handrails and grabrails, and drop-down rails that are easy to operate, are recommended. Consider texture to aid grip.

- Emergency alarm systems should be provided. These should be audible as well as visual. The call signal outside the compartment should be located so that it can be easily seen and heard by those able to give assistance. Pull-cords should extend to 100mm above floor level and be easy to grip.

- Coat hooks and mirrors should be fixed at heights usable by standing and seated users. The recommended height for a coat hook is 1200mm and for mirrors 600–1600mm.

- Fittings such as radiators, vending machines, sanitary disposal units and waste paper bins should be set at appropriate heights and recessed where possible so as not to obstruct transfer space or manoeuvrability.

- Sink plumbing returned to the wall (rather than run to the floor) is preferred as this leaves more clear space below the hand washbasin.

- The boxing-in of pipes should be carefully considered so as not to compromise manoeuvring space.

WCs

- An emergency light should be provided within the compartment to ensure that a person is not left in the dark during a power failure.

For guidance on wheelchair-accessible changing and shower facilities and bathrooms, see AD M or BS 8300.

Figure 36
Unisex accessible corner WC

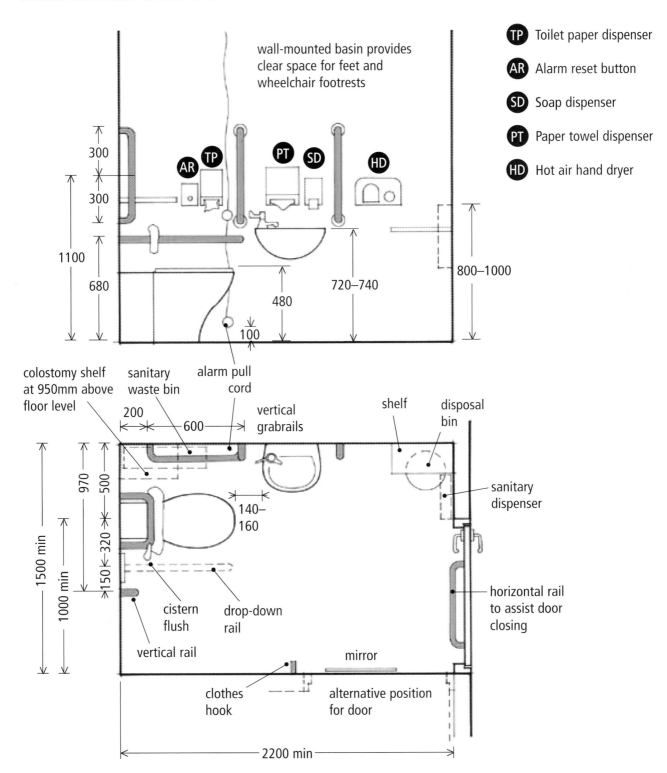

TP Toilet paper dispenser

AR Alarm reset button

SD Soap dispenser

PT Paper towel dispenser

HD Hot air hand dryer

Seating

General guidance on seating for occasional use is given here.

- Seats should be provided at intervals along long routes or where waiting is likely.

- Seats should be stable and provided in a range of heights. BS 8300 recommends between 450 and 475mm for fixed seating. In larger buildings where more seating is provided, consider a wider range of seat heights from 420 to 580mm and 'perch' seats at 650 to 800mm on long routes or in short-stay waiting areas.

- A mixture of fixed and loose seating provides flexibility of use of space.

- A mixture of seating with and without armrests should be provided.

- In waiting areas there should be space for a wheelchair user to pull up alongside a seated companion. One space within or at the end of a block of seating could be provided for an assistance dog to rest.

- Seating should contrast in colour and luminance with surrounding surfaces.

For more detailed guidance on seating see BS 8300. For guidance on audience or spectator seating in various building types, see AD M, BS 8300 and Sport England's *Access for Disabled People.*

Fixtures, fittings and services

Counters and service desks

Counters and service desks should be designed so that they can be accessed and used – on both staff and customer sides – by as wide range of people as possible.

- Counters and desks should be set at a height suitable for seated and standing users, with high and low sections where possible (see *Figure 37*) and with sufficient clear manoeuvring space in front (see *Figure 38*).

- Access for wheelchair users should be provided to both staff and visitor sides of the counter. For clear manoeuvring space see *Figure 38*.

- There should be sufficient counter space to allow people to write or sign documents.

- An upstanding lip at the edge of the counter, if well detailed, can assist in picking up tickets or loose change.

Figure 37
Counters/service desks

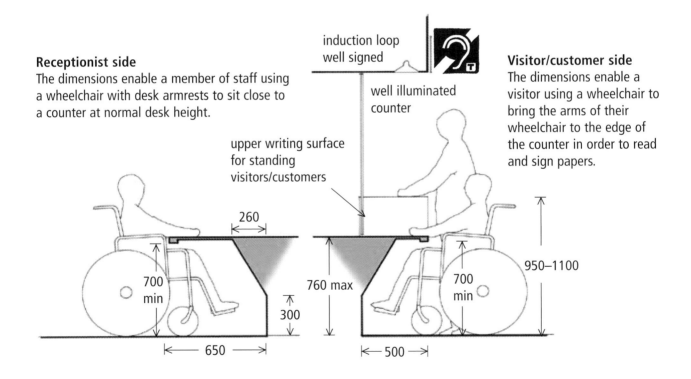

Receptionist side
The dimensions enable a member of staff using a wheelchair with desk armrests to sit close to a counter at normal desk height.

induction loop well signed

upper writing surface for standing visitors/customers

well illuminated counter

Visitor/customer side
The dimensions enable a visitor using a wheelchair to bring the arms of their wheelchair to the edge of the counter in order to read and sign papers.

260
700 min
300
650
760 max
500
700 min
950–1100

Counters and service desks

Counters and service desks

- Contrast between objects and surface is helpful. Top of counter should contrast with edge.

- All exposed edges and corners should be well rounded.

- Avoid positioning service desks in front of windows where bright sunshine will cause the user's face to be silhouetted and hence difficult to lip-read or follow sign language. Similarly, avoid confusing backgrounds such as strong patterns.

- Lighting should assist lip-reading on both sides of the counter.

- Induction loops should serve staff and visitors. There should be clear signs indicating where loops are fitted.

- Speech enhancement and induction loop systems fitted at counters with glazed screens or where there is background noise will help people with hearing aids.

- Provision of seats near low counters could be considered.

Figure 38
Space dimensions in front of counter/service desk

clear manoeuvring space:
A: counter/desktop without knee recess
B: counter/desktop with knee recess

a low-level counter 1800mm wide will accommodate two wheelchair users alongside each other or facing each other across the counter diagonally

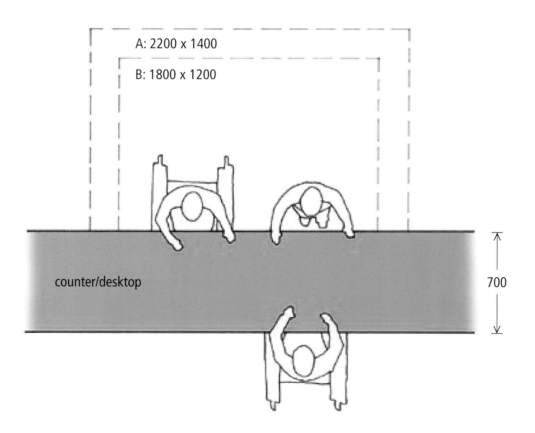

A: 2200 x 1400

B: 1800 x 1200

counter/desktop

700

Telephones

In buildings where telephones are provided for the public, at least one accessible telephone should be provided.

- If possible, locate telephones where background noise levels are minimal.

- Telephones should be fixed at a height that allows wheelchair users to read any visual display panels and to use the telephone with ease (see *Figure 39*).

- If telephones are fixed at a low height, seats should be provided.

- Where several telephones are provided, a range of fixing heights to suit standing and seated users should be adopted.

- A textphone should be provided, clearly indicated by the standard symbol (see *Figure 42*).

- An induction coupler fitted to a telephone enables it to be used by someone with a hearing aid. Such telephones should have variable volume controls and be identified by the standard symbol (see *Figure 42*).

Figure 39
Accessible telephones

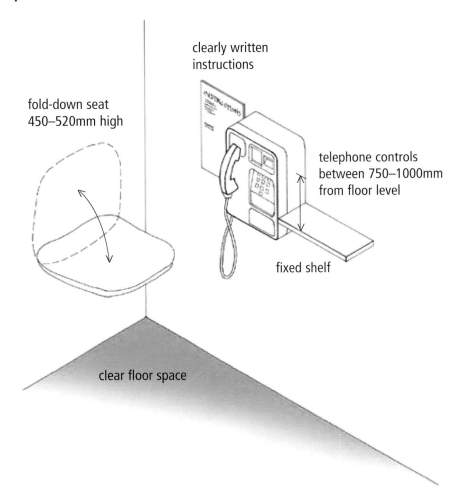

fold-down seat
450–520mm high

clearly written
instructions

telephone controls
between 750–1000mm
from floor level

fixed shelf

clear floor space

Wayfinding, information and signs

Buildings designed with a logical layout can directly assist wayfinding, particularly for people with sight impairments and people with learning difficulties, as well as facilitating means of escape. Additional information can be conveyed through colour, communication systems, maps, models and guides.

- Clearly audible public address systems should be supplemented by visual information (see also p 59 *Acoustics*).

- Colour can be used to signal where certain features can be found within a building. For example, all walls within core areas containing stairs, lifts and WCs could be painted a particular colour to help orientation.

- Visual information can be provided by distinguishing floor, wall and ceiling planes, door surrounds and decorative features.

- Tactile maps and models of the interior layout of buildings – particularly those of architectural interest – aid the comprehension of the building for those with sight impairments.

- When complex information is being provided, audio or BSL-interpreted guides should also be considered.

- Where a building relies upon its own vocabulary of textured surfaces to convey information to people with sight impairments, a key should be provided at a central information point.

Signs

- Location of signs should be part of the process of planning the building. They should be placed in a logical position and be obviously identifiable.

- Signs are difficult to identify and read if they are positioned against a background of low-level sunlight or artificial light.

- The signboard should contrast with the background against which it is seen, and the lettering should contrast with the sign board.

- Directional signs should be situated so that they do not cause obstruction and are well lit. They should be positioned at high level in areas of buildings that are likely to be crowded.

- Informational signs to be read at close range should be located at a suitable height. The recommended range for a wheelchair user is 1000–1100mm and for somebody standing 1400–1700mm.

Figure 40
Height and position of signs

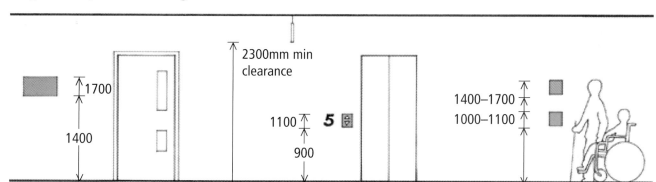

Wayfinding, information and signs

- Signs need to be simple, short, consistent and easily understood using prescribed typefaces, colour and graphic devices.

- Signs are more easily read if the wording starts with a capital letter and is followed by lower case lettering.

- Factors which determine the legibility of signs include the contrast between the text colour and the background colour, the contrast between the sign itself and the background surfaces, and lighting conditions.

- To minimise glare, avoid reflective glass and ensure that the sign has a matt surface.

- Symbols should be used to supplement written signs (see *Figure 42*).

- Tactile signs (such as embossed letters, raised pictograms and direction arrows) should only be used where they can be easily reached, for example lift controls, door numbers, lockers and WC doors.

For more detailed guidance on use of signs in buildings, see BS 8300 and the *Sign Design Guide* published by JMU and the Sign Design Society.

Figure 41
Sign design detail

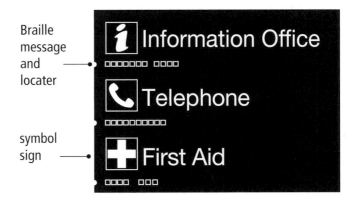

Braille message and locater

symbol sign

arrows and text aligned towards direction of travel

- locations listed and left-aligned where no arrows
- use of capitals and lower case text
- effective contrast between text and background

Figure 42
Standard public information symbols

international symbol of access, indicating accessible routes and facilities

facilities for blind or partially sighted people

equipment to enhance microphone sound for people whose hearing aid is fitted with a 'T' switch

equipment to enhance microphone sound through an infrared receiver

text telephone facilities

Alarms

It is important that people with visual or hearing impairments can be alerted in case of emergency.

- Consideration should be given to visual alarms or vibrating pager systems (but note that certain types of strobe light alarm systems may induce seizures in some people).

- Use of emergency alarms must be backed up by a suitable evacuation strategy for all occupants, both staff and visitors, taking into account all disabilities. See p 63 *Means of escape.*

Alarms

Switches and controls

The location and detailing of switches and controls should take into account ease of operation, height, distance from corners, visibility and unobstructed access.

• See *Figure 43* for heights of various different kinds of switches, controls and sockets.

• The operation of switches, sockets and controls should not require the simultaneous use of both hands. Large switch pads are recommended.

• Avoid flushed or recessed controls, as these are not accessible to people with limited dexterity.

• Colour and tonal contrast should be used to ensure controls are distinguishable from their background.

• Ensure that switched socket outlets, mains and circuit isolator switches indicate clearly whether they are 'on' or 'off' (red and green colour indication, if used, should be supplemented by text or pictogram indication).

• Consider the use of tactile buttons and controls. These should be embossed, not engraved.

Figure 43
Height of switches and controls

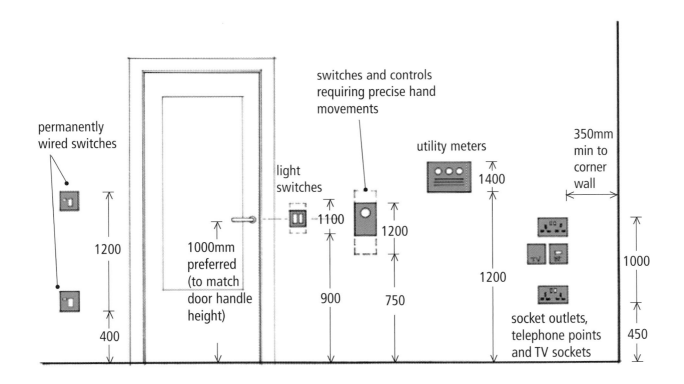

Lighting

Good lighting is essential for everyone for visibility and safety. Lighting systems can be used to accentuate interior colour, tone and texture scheme.

- All lighting, including natural light, should be controllable and adjustable where possible to suit the needs of the individual.

- Good light levels are particularly important in potentially hazardous areas such as stair wells or changes in level along a route.

- Passive infrared sensors can be used to detect dim light and activate booster lighting.

- Keeping windows, blinds and lamps clean maximises the amount of light available.

- Lights should be positioned where they do not cause glare, reflection, confusing shadows or pools of light and dark.

- Positioning lighting in unusual or unexpected places can create shadows and misleading visual effects.

- Uplighters placed above a standing person's eye level can deliver comfortable, glare-free illumination.

- Some fluorescent lights create a magnetic field which can cause a hum in hearing aids. Lighting of this type should be specified with care where it cannot inconvenience people with hearing impairments.

- Artificial lighting should be compatible with other electronic and radio frequency installations.

- Consider how different types of lighting affect colours and contrast, which may cause problems for people with visual impairments.

For further guidance see CIBSE *Code for Lighting* and BS 8300.

Acoustics

Consideration of the acoustic properties of buildings, as well as the specification of hearing enhancement systems, can benefit people with hearing impairments.

- In order to allow people with hearing impairments to maximise their residual hearing, it is important to keep background noise to a minimum.

- However, sounds can be useful for people with visual impairments. For example, the sound of a lift arrival bell locates the lift, and being able to hear footsteps informs that someone is approaching.

Noise reduction

- Consider areas where communication will be important, such as reception desks. Locate these away from potentially noisy areas.

- Provide adequate sound insulation to minimise intrusive noise, both from outside and within the building.

- Separate quiet and noisy areas of buildings with a buffer zone.

- Avoid too many hard surfaces, which cause problems for people with hearing impairments.

- Supplementary heating units should be chosen with a view to minimising background noise, which can be distracting and tiring for people with hearing impairments.

- Air conditioning units and extractor fans create a lot of background noise. They should be regularly maintained in order to reduce noise due to wear.

- The main power supply cable to a building generates a considerable magnetic field, which can cause a loud hum in hearing aids. Care should be taken to route the cable away from public spaces.

- Computers, overhead and slide projectors and lighting can create background noise and interfere with hearing aids.

Hearing enhancement systems

- AD M requires that hearing enhancement systems be installed in rooms and spaces designed for meetings, lectures, classes, performances, spectator sports or films, and at service or reception counters where they are situated in noisy areas or are behind glazed screens. The presence of an induction loop or infrared system should be indicated by the standard symbol.

Induction loops

- Induction loops convert sound via a microphone into a varying magnetic field, which is converted back to amplified sound by an individual's hearing aid (where a 'T' switch is fitted). Loops help to cut out extraneous background noise.

- Induction loops should be fitted wherever information is given verbally: airports, railway stations, box offices, ticket counters, banks, post offices, churches, meeting rooms, cinemas and theatres.

- Further technical advice should be sought from induction loop system manufacturers. Some systems may allow sound to be picked up by hearing aid users in adjacent rooms – this is called overlap. This may be a problem in multi-screen cinemas, adjacent classrooms, or where confidentiality is required. Large amounts of metal within a building can also reduce the effectiveness of the loop system.

Acoustics

Infrared systems

- Infrared systems work on different principles by converting a sound source into an infrared light signal, and require special receiving headsets. This system is more suitable for controlled areas such as cinemas, theatres and lecture rooms, where headsets can be borrowed from a central source. The system is of particular value where confidentiality is important. As the technology is based on light, sound cannot be picked up outside the room in which the infrared signals are generated.

- Infrared systems cannot be used externally.

FM radio systems

- FM radio systems can be used in situations where a loop, infrared or sound reinforcement system is not available. Using a licence-exempt FM radio link, the transmitter and receivers are lightweight and compact and can be worn under clothing. Receiver units have a thumb-wheel volume control, and both units have power 'on' indicators.

- The systems can be used with a supplied earphone/headphones or with a neckloop (hearing aid switched to 'T') for extra seclusion and clearer sound. The range is up to 30m. This type of system is particularly suitable for training and educational purposes.

Building management checklist

Accessibility cannot be guaranteed by good design alone. How a building is managed in its day-to-day running will have a huge impact on how easy it is to use by disabled people. For example, a spacious lift lobby with plenty of room for a wheelchair user to reverse into the lift is rendered useless if left full of boxes of stationery. Installing an induction loop in a theatre or meeting room is only useful if management advertises its presence and staff know how to use it.

Checklist

It is important that those involved in making a building accessible – whether new or existing – contribute to the drafting of a building management manual, which can be updated and added to as required and linked to any Access Statement. In response to duties under the DDA, and to achieve good practice in the management of buildings generally, the following building management and maintenance issues should be considered.

Car parking – ensure that non-disabled drivers do not occupy bays intended for disabled people.

Bicycles – ensure that bicycles are not left across access routes or chained to the handrails of steps or ramps.

Routes and external paving surfaces – ensure that external routes, ramps and steps are kept clean, unobstructed and free of surface water, snow and ice and of algae growth.

Vegetation/planting – ensure that planted borders, shrubs, bushes and trees are not allowed to grow to an extent whereby they obstruct paving, entrances, routes, signs or the spread of light.

Doors – ensure that door closers are regularly maintained, door ironmongery is kept clean and free-moving, side-hung doors accompanying revolving doors are not kept locked.

Door opening – ensure that doors are easy to use. Where an opening force at the leading edge of a door of 20 newtons cannot be achieved, options to consider include:

- a door can be held open (on magnetic closers linked to the fire alarm if it is a fire door)
- the door closer can be removed if it is not required (though fire containment must be the priority)
- the door can be automated
- assistance can be provided as and when required (this option is a last resort as it results in a lack of independent access)

Horizontal circulation – ensure that spaces required for wheelchair manoeuvres are not obstructed by deliveries or storage and ensure access between movable tables, for example in refreshment areas.

Vertical circulation – ensure that lifts are regularly checked to see that the lift car floor aligns with the structural floor, that short-rise lifts are not abused by people using them as goods lifts and that portable ramps are available where needed.

WCs – ensure that supplies of toilet tissue and paper towels are regularly replenished, that the waste bin is not left in transfer spaces, and that the WC is not used as an unofficial storage area.

Signs – ensure that new signs integrate with the existing signage, that signs are replaced correctly when removed for

Building management checklist

redecoration, and that temporary signs are removed when no longer relevant.

Maps and models – ensure that maps and models of building interiors are updated when departments move offices within the building.

Hearing enhancement systems – ensure that installations are advertised and regularly checked, and that staff are properly trained.

Alarms and security – ensure that alarm systems, including those in WCs, are regularly checked and that new staff are trained in alarm response procedures.

Surfaces – ensure that cleaning and polishing does not render slip-resistant surfaces slippery. Ensure that the junctions between different flooring materials do not become worn, presenting a tripping hazard. Ensure that, when flooring is renewed, like is replaced by like. Ensuring that the redecoration of interiors does not compromise a carefully selected colour scheme designed to impart information to people with poor sight or impair contrast with features such as door frames, control panels or signs.

Lighting – ensure that windows, lamps and blinds are kept clean in order to maximise available light. Ensuring that blown light bulbs are swiftly replaced.

Information – ensure that up-to-date information is available on the accessibility of the building, on the equipment available, on the assistance available in order to overcome any barriers, and on the nearest accessible parking and accessible WCs if these are not provided.

Policy issues – including reviewing allocation of parking spaces, number of disabled people needing facilities, signage policy, staff training and evacuation procedures. Commissioning access audits and ensuring that access improvements are incorporated wherever possible in maintenance and refurbishment work.

Means of escape

Means of escape is a crucial subject area that should be considered at the same time as access. *Designing for Accessibility* does not attempt to cover emergency egress from buildings in the same degree of detail as access to and within buildings.

The design of a building alone cannot ensure safety for the occupants in the case of a fire or other emergency. Means of escape strategies should be devised by the building's management in conjunction with designers, fire officers, access consultants and building users in order to ensure safe, swift and orderly evacuation for all. Escape strategies for disabled building users may differ from those for able-bodied building users according to the amount of assistance they require in order to leave the building.

Detailed information on means of escape is given in Part 8 of BS 5588:1988 *Fire Precautions in the Design, Construction and Use of Buildings – Code of practice for means of escape for disabled people.* This document considers the concepts of horizontal and vertical escape, proposing that disabled people evacuate themselves as far as possible horizontally to a fire-protected refuge space on or near the escape stairs. From there they can be evacuated vertically with the required assistance by the building management or fire brigade. It states that lifts can be used to assist in the evacuation of disabled building users if they are encased within a fire-protected shaft and have their own independent electrical supply and control panel. Appendices give guidance on evacuation techniques.

The safe and competent evacuation of disabled employees and other known, regular building users depends to a large part upon the creation of bespoke personal emergency egress plans that take into account the difficulties of the building, people's requirements for assistance, and the abilities of colleagues in giving that assistance.

Generic emergency evacuation plans can be devised to meet the needs of visitors. These will be fundamentally suited for the evacuation of wheelchair users or ambulant disabled people or people with visual impairments, and will facilitate the safe evacuation of disabled visitors whose needs cannot be identified in advance.

Means of escape

Organisations

British Standards Institution (BSI)
389 Chiswick High Road
London W4 4AL
Tel: 020 8996 9000
Fax: 020 8996 7001
Email: cservices@bsi-global.com
Website: www.bsi.org.uk

Publishes British Standards including BS 8300:2001 *Design of buildings and their approaches to meet the needs of disabled people – Code of practice.*

Centre for Accessible Environments
Nutmeg House
60 Gainsford Street
London SE1 2NY
Tel/textphone: 020 7357 8182
Fax: 020 7357 8183
Email: info@cae.org.uk
Website: www.cae.org.uk

Provides technical information, training and consultancy on making buildings accessible to all users, including disabled and older people and carers of young children.

Department for Work and Pensions
Disability Unit
Level 6
Adelphi
1-11 John Adam Street
London WC2N 6HT
Tel: 020 7712 2171
Fax: 020 7712 2386
Website: www.dwp.gov.uk and www.disability.gov.uk

Responsible for the Government's welfare reform agenda, supports disabled people and their carers, disability benefits and disability civil rights issues.

Disability Rights Commission
DRC Helpline
Freepost MID 02164
Stratford-upon-Avon CV37 9BR
Tel: 08457 622 633
Textphone: 08457 622 644
Fax: 08457 778 878
Email: enquiry@drc-gb.org
Website: www.drc.org.uk

Publishes codes of practice and other guidance related to the DDA.

The Equality Commission for Northern Ireland
Equality House
7-9 Shaftesbury Square
Belfast BT2 7DP
Tel: 028 90 500600
Fax: 028 90 248687
Textphone: 028 90 500589
Email: information@equalityni.org

Works towards the elimination of discrimination and keeps the relevant legislation under review.

Employers' Forum on Disability
Nutmeg House
60 Gainsford Street
London SE1 2NY
Tel: 020 7403 3020
Textphone: 020 7403 0040
Fax: 020 7403 0404
Email: enquiries@employers-forum.co.uk
Website: www.employers-forum.co.uk

Represents and advises member companies on disability issues, plus information on good practice available free to all businesses.

The Mobility and Inclusion Unit
Department for Transport
Zone 1/18, Great Minster House
76 Marsham Street
London SW1P 4DR
Tel: 020 7944 8300
Fax: 020 7944 6589

Organisations

Email: miu@dft.gsi.gov.uk
Website: www.mobility-unit.dft.gov.uk

Research, information and policy advice.

National Register of Access Consultants
Nutmeg House
60 Gainsford Street
London SE1 2NY
Tel: 020 7234 0434
Textphone: 020 7357 8182
Fax: 020 7357 8182
Email: info@nrac.org.uk
Website: www.nrac.org.uk

Enables clients quickly and easily to locate suitable auditors or consultants, and provides a quality standard for those advising on the accessibility of the built environment for disabled people.

Royal Institute of British Architects (RIBA)
66 Portland Place
London W1B 1AD
Public information line: 0906 302 0400
Tel: 020 7580 5533
Fax: 020 7255 1541
Email: info@inst.riba.org
Website: www.architecture.com

The RIBA advances architecture by demonstrating benefit to society and excellence in the profession.

Royal National Institute of the Blind (RNIB)
105 Judd Street
London W1H 9NE
Tel: 020 7388 1266
Fax: 020 7388 2034
Email: helpline@rnib.org.uk
Website: www.rnib.org.uk

Help, advice and support for people with serious visual impairments.

Royal National Institute for Deaf People (RNID)
19-23 Featherstone Street
London EC1Y 8SL
National information line: 0808 808 0123
Tel: 020 7296 8000
Textphone: 020 7296 8199
Email: informationline@rnid.org.uk
Website: www.rnid.org.uk

Provides consultancy on the environmental needs of people with hearing impairments.

Scottish Executive Development Department
Victoria Quay
Edinburgh EH6 6QQ
Tel: 0131 556 8400
Textphone: 0131 244 1829
Fax: 0131 244 8240
Email: ceu@scotland.gov.uk
Website: www.scotland.gov.uk

For information on the Scottish Technical Standards.

The Stationery Office Ltd
PO Box 29
Duke Street
Norwich NR3 1GN
Tel: 0870 600 5522
Fax: 0870 600 5533
Email: services@tso.co.uk
Online ordering:
www.tso.co.uk/bookshop

Sells printed versions of any item of legislation or any other official publication previously published by HMSO.

Publications

Legislation, standards and codes of practice

The Building Regulations 2000 Approved Document M: Access to and use of buildings (England and Wales)
Office of the Deputy Prime Minister
The Stationery Office, 2003

The Building Regulations (Northern Ireland) 2000 Technical booklet R: Access and facilities for disabled people
Great Britain Department of Finance and Personnel (Northern Ireland)
The Stationery Office, 2001

Scottish Executive Technical Standard, 6th Amendment
Scottish Executive
The Stationery Office, 2001

BS 8300:2001 Design of buildings and their approaches to meet the needs of disabled people – Code of practice
The British Standards Institution, 2001

BS 5588:Part 8:1988 Fire Precautions in the Design, Construction and Use of Buildings – Code of practice for means of escape for disabled people
The British Standards Institution, 1988

BS 6440:1999 Powered lifting platforms for use by disabled persons – Code of practice
The British Standards Institution, 1999

BS EN 81-70:2003 Safety rules for the construction and installation of lifts – Particular applications for passenger and goods passenger lifts
The British Standards Institution, 2003

Disability Discrimination Act 1995
The Stationery Office, 1995

Special Educational Needs and Disability Act 2001
The Stationery Office, 2001

Code of Practice for the Elimination of Discrimination in the Field of Employment against Disabled Persons or Persons who have had a Disability
Disability Rights Commission
The Stationery Office, 1996

Code of Practice Rights of Access to Goods, Facilities, Services and Premises
Disability Rights Commission
The Stationery Office, 2002

Code of Practice for providers of Post-16 education and related services
Disability Rights Commission
The Stationery Office, 2002

Code of Practice for Schools
Disability Rights Commission
The Stationery Office, 2002

Draft Code of Practice – Employment and Occupation
Disability Rights Commission, 2003

Draft Code of Practice – Trade Organisations and Qualification Bodies
Disability Rights Commission, 2003

Publications

Other publications

Access Audits: a guide and checklist for appraising the accessibility of public buildings
CAE, 2003
Includes guidance notes, series of checklists, film *Access Audits: a planning tool for businesses* and design guide for public buildings *Designing for Accessibility.*

Access Audits: a planning tool for businesses
CAE, 2003
Prize-winning film which explains what an access audit is and how its recommendations can be used to improve a business's premises and customer services. Available on VHS cassette, CD ROM and DVD, with subtitles or BSL.

Access Audit Price Guide 2002 for work in relation to the Disability Discrimination Act
Building Cost Information Service Ltd, The Royal Institution of Chartered Surveyors, 2002
Clear, concise, specialist guidance on the costs of alteration works and improvements that may be required to existing premises as a consequence of the reforms being brought about by the DDA and changes to AD M.

Access for Disabled People
Sport England, 2002
Design guidance note including a series of checklists for auditing sports buildings.

Access to ATMs: UK design guidelines
by Robert Feeney
CAE, 2002
Design principles and guidance for those who design, manufacture, install and maintain ATMs.

Building Sight
by Peter Barker, Jon Barrick, Rod Wilson
HMSO in association with the Royal National Institute of the Blind
RNIB, 1995
A handbook of building and interior design solutions to include the needs of visually impaired people.

Code for Lighting
Chartered Institution of Building Services Engineers (CIBSE), 2000
Detailed guidance on all aspects of lighting.

A Design Guide for the Use of Colour and Contrast to Improve the Built Environment for Visually Impaired People
Dulux Technical Group, ICI Paints, 1997

Disabled Access to Facilities: a practical and comprehensive guide to a service provider's duties under Part III (2004) of the Disability Discrimination Act 1995
FM Law Series
by Ian Waterman and Janet A Bell, Access Matters UK Ltd
Butterworths Tolley Lexis Nexis, 2002

Disability: Making Building Accessible – Special Report
Edited by Keith Bright
Workplace Law Network, 2003

Disability Portfolio
Resource: The Council for Museums, Archives and Libraries, 2003
Series of 12 guides on how to meet the needs of disabled people as users and staff in museums, archives and libraries including guides on the DDA, Audits and Accessible Environments.
www.resource.gov.uk/action/learnacc/o oaccess_03.asp

Publications

Easy Access to Historic Properties
English Heritage, 1995 (now out of print; new edition expected to be published in 2004)
Guidance in relation to achieving access in historic buildings.

Good Loo Design Guide
CAE/RIBA Enterprises, 2004
Authoritative design guidance on WCs that meet the requirement of all users.

Guidance on Access Statements
(draft title)
Disability Rights Commission, CAE and RIBA Enterprises, to be published 2004

Guidance on the use of Tactile Paving Surfaces
DTLR Mobility and Inclusion Unit, 1999

Inclusive Mobility: a guide to best practice on access to pedestrian and transport infrastructure
by Philip R Oxley, Cranfield Centre for Logistics and Transportation Department for Transport Mobility and Inclusion Unit, 2002

Inclusive Projects: a guide to best practice on preparing and delivering project briefs to secure access
Disabled Persons Transport Advisory Committee, Department of Transport 2003

Inclusive School Design – Accommodating pupils with special educational needs and disabilities in mainstream schools
Department for Education and Employment
The Stationery Office, 2001

Planning and Access for Disabled People – A Good Practice Guide
Office of the Deputy Prime Minister, 2003
How to ensure that the town and country planning system in England successfully and consistently delivers inclusive environments as an integral part of the development process.

Sign Design Guide
by Peter Parker and June Fraser
JMU and the Sign Design Society, 2000
A guide to inclusive signage.

Centre for Accessible Environments

The Centre for Accessible Environments is an information provider and a forum for collaborative dialogue between providers and users on how the built environment can best be made or modified to achieve inclusion by design.

Founded in 1969, registered as a charity in 1976, the Centre is the acknowledged centre of excellence on the practicalities of designing for accessibility. As a charity, we have a mission to share our knowledge and expertise. Our services include information, training, consultancy and publications.

RIBA Enterprises

RIBA Enterprises is a leading provider of information in the fields of architecture and construction for specifiers and manufacturers, as well as for engineers, surveyors, construction lawyers, contractors, academics and students.

We are committed to delivering a wide range of products and services each year, to the highest quality, in practice management, construction law, design, specifying, construction contracts, forms of appointment and associated guidance and monographs.

With a comprehensive range of publications, products and services, and a history spanning more than 30 years, RIBA Enterprises is the perfect partner to provide solutions to all your business, professional and academic needs.

Index